PUBLIC AND PRIVATE MORALITY

"A very readable, helpful application of King David's life to the moral struggles, both public and private, of our own day."

Ronald J. Sider, President, Evangelicals for Social Action

"In his latest book Tom Houston has distilled the wisdom of David and married it with his own insights and profound experience of Christian leadership.

He has understood the lessons of leadership that King David learned and shares them with those who would exercise Christian leadership in the church of the 21st century.

While this is a short book it is one that repays reading many times and will prove to be a invaluable manual and resource of spiritual principles to anyone who reads it is an easy book to commend, though it will bring pointed challenges to the life of the reader."

Rob Norris, Fourth Presbyterian Church, Bethsaida, Maryland

"Tom Houston's timely book features impeccable Biblical scholarship on the Davidic era thoughtfully applied to the dilemmas and temptations that test contemporary consciences. King David comes alive in these pages as a pathfinder whose human failures and spiritual recoveries are highly relevant to public and private morality in the 21st century. Warmly recommended."

Jonathan Aitken,
Author of biographies of Richard Nixon and Charles Colson

PUBLIC AND PRIVATE MORALITY

REFLECTIONS FOR TODAY'S LEADERS ON KING DAVID

TOM HOUSTON

CHRISTIAN FOCUS

Tom Houston is a retired Scot and resident with his wife Hazle in Oxford, England. He served as a pastor for 20 years in Scotland and Nairobi, Kenya and then went on to serve with the British and Foreign Bible Society, World Vision and the Lausanne Committee for World Evangelisation until his retirement in 1998.

© Tom Houston 2006

ISBN 1-85792-967-5 (10)
ISBN 978-1-85792-967-6 (13)

10 9 8 7 6 5 4 3 2 1

Published in 2006
by
Christian Focus Publications,
Geanies House, Fearn, Ross-shire,
IV20 1TW, Great Britain.

www.christianfocus.com

Cover Design by
Danie Van Straaten

Printed by Nørhaven Paperback A/S

Contents

Introduction

Public and Private Morality are themes often discussed today. Should marital infidelity disqualify a person from public office? Should the private lives of public figures be open to press scrutiny? Should there be any distinction at all between private and public morality? Should morality come into the political equation at all? There is never much agreement when the subjects come up. Could it be that there might be help from the past for this very modern dilemma?

If we go back 3,000 years we find a unique case study. A total beginner gets jolted in his teens into a pathway that leads to leadership. He has to learn everything from scratch. There was no help from his family. His country had never really had a king and were not sure that they wanted one. The person who was trying to be king was not making a very good job of it.

I am referring to David, the first real King of Israel, around 1000 BC. His path to power was further complicated by the fact that the examples of kings among the surrounding peoples were precisely what he should not be following. He was on his own and had to fumble his way forward to leadership. He did it remarkably well, given where he started from.

All he had to go on was the cultural and religious history of his people, the Israelites, and they were really different from the other people in the region. For one thing, they were the first people to believe in only one God. They were the original monotheists. All their neighbours, without exception, worshipped many gods who each represented something in nature, like the sun, the moon, sex, fertility or the seasons.

The LORD that Israel believed in was above and outside all that. He had created everything in the first place and sustained all the natural processes. He even controlled what happened in history, especially their own, sometimes using the weather and other natural phenomena to do so. They believed that he made Israel his own people, brought them from slavery in Egypt and had promised them the land of Canaan where they now lived. He was all powerful, completely just and merciful.

People are made in the image of God. They are like him. He is like them. This is their value. This is their dignity. Men and women bear his likeness, so God is personal.

Now the Israelites were divided among themselves and harassed and oppressed by neighbours like the Philistines. Theirs was not a happy lot. So, the challenge set before David was to carve out a path to become king of Israel and then create a concept of leadership that would work, with practically no precedent to follow.

The materials from which we are to derive this astonishingly detailed story are of three kinds. There are the two books of Samuel in the Bible. These are among the first examples of historical narrative that exist anywhere in the world. They were written relatively soon after the events they describe, or at least the writers were able to draw on sources that were near to these events. We are also indebted to the two books of Chronicles that cover the same ground from a different angle and were written several centuries later and after Israel had ceased to be a kingdom at all. Many psalms were also written by our subject. Out of the 150 psalms in the Bible 73 have a title that ascribes them to David. This provides an internal, subjective side to the story that lies alongside the historical material and completes the life picture of our subject. I shall take these texts as they stand and put the most plausible construction on the material. It is my aim as much as possible to let the story do the talking.

The moral issues of today are not the same as they were in Palestine in 1000 BC. They were not abstractly divided into public and private.

Life was seen as a whole. The standards of behaviour were framed in the Ten Commandments, but there was room for amendment of life even after the standards were broken. To do justice to this, I have used the title, 'Beyond Public and Private Morality.'

To try and bridge this cultural gap between then and now, I will indicate the possible equivalent issues that arise today on a facing page at the beginning of each chapter. In the story I will try to stick to the original context and let the readers make their own applications.

This is a book for general readers with access to a Bible. They can check and verify from the appropriate sections of the Bible nearly all they read here. The treatment may be imaginative but it is not implausible. There should not be any need to consult the huge corpus of scholarly work that has been written about this story. If they do consult it, they will find that the author is not unfamiliar with the very wide range of opinion that scholars have expressed, but only uses what elucidates the story as we have it.

There is no doubt that this person, David, became a great influence on later Israelite history and thought. He is the key to understanding some important themes in the New Testament. I have tried not to read back this later influence into these chapters but have included two additional notes to the appropriate chapters where the story does need carrying forward.

TODAY'S CHALLENGES:

Coping in a dysfunctional family.
Handling youthful big ideas.

'He chose his servant David;
he took him from the pastures,
where he looked after his flocks,
and he made him king of Israel...'
(Ps. 78:70)

1

A Whisper of Great Things to Come

1 Samuel 16

SMALL BEGINNINGS

David, our subject, arrived on the scene some years before 1000 BC. That places him about four centuries after Moses and the exodus from Egypt and 400 years before the Jews were driven into exile in Babylon (Matt. 1:17).

Palestine is a small country, about 145 miles from north to south and about 60 miles from the Mediterranean in the east to the desert in the west. It is about the size of Wales in the UK or the small state of Massachusetts in USA. In Africa it would match The Gambia, in Latin America, Belize, and in Asia it would be smaller than Taiwan.

David was from the tribe of Judah; that made him a Jew. Judah was the largest in numbers and in territory of the twelve tribes of Israel. Judah occupied a little more than a quarter of the land mass in the south of the country. So, we are not talking big history here and yet the implications for world history proved to be very great indeed.

David came from a historically significant family in Bethlehem in Judah (Ruth 4:18-22). He was the youngest son in a family of eight sons and two daughters.

UNCERTAIN TIMES

The political context of the area had been a mess for centuries. There were a number of tribes and city states that were nominally subject to the great Egyptian Empire in the south. That did not prevent them from producing warlords and engaging in internecine skirmishes for the purposes of plunder, cattle thieving and control of such fertile land as there was.

Recently there had been some successful moves to get the Israelite act together. First there was a prophet, Samuel, who worked at establishing some semblance of law and order and unity and who kept at bay the principal enemy, the warlike Philistines at the coast. Then the people demanded to have a king like other nations and Samuel anointed their tallest man, Saul, as king. After some initial success Saul was proving to be an erratic leader and there was a serious split between him and the prophet Samuel. This is where our story begins.

A SECRET CEREMONY

In the middle of this dispute Samuel arrived unexpectedly in Bethlehem and announced to the elders of the place that he was there to offer a special sacrifice at which he wanted Jesse and his family to be present. Everyone was very nervous in case Saul should hear that Samuel had been there and kill them for disloyalty. Jesse and his family were particularly concerned when they seemed to be marked out for special attention.

The altar was made ready, the fire lit and the animal slaughtered. Samuel was paying special attention to the sons of Jesse. What those present did not know was that Samuel had been ordered by God to go to Bethlehem to pick a successor to King Saul from the household of one of their leading families.

Broad-shouldered, tall, handsome, Jesse's sons came to be presented to Samuel. The strong smell of the burning sacrifice filled the air. 'This man is surely the one God has chosen', thought Samuel as he saw Jesse's oldest son Eliab approach the heifer on the stone altar. Muscles rippled under Eliab's tunic; he gave a confident smile to Samuel, who stood ready to anoint the next king over Israel. Even as Samuel tightened his grip on the horn of oil, however, the voice of God stopped him. 'Pay no attention to how tall and handsome he is… Man looks at the outward appearance, but I look at the heart' (1 Sam. 16:6-7). Samuel motioned Eliab to move on. Surprised, perhaps somewhat piqued, he passed by the altar, and Jesse called Abinadab. 'No, the LORD hasn't chosen him either.' Abinadab passed by the altar and Jesse called Shammah. 'No, the LORD hasn't chosen him either.' Shammah passed by the altar, and Jesse called his remaining sons. 'No, the LORD hasn't chosen any of these' (1 Sam. 16:8-10). With ritual regularity the refrain sounded in Samuel's heart, as one by one Jesse's sons were introduced to Samuel until there were none left.

'Have you any more sons?' asked Samuel tersely. Jesse mentioned David, hardly worth bothering about, since he was just a teenager tending the sheep. But Samuel cut him short with a peremptory command: 'Tell him to come here… We won't offer the sacrifice until he comes' (1 Sam. 16:11). The seven sons of Jesse exchanged quizzical glances. Impatience rose in Eliab's face, but only the sound of sizzling fat from the roasting heifer dropping on the hot stones broke the silence as Samuel awaited the approach of David.

Then David stood there before the altar, with a ruddy complexion and handsome features like the rest. He was skilled at the harp, well-spoken, as yet untested in battle but brave like his brothers. Immediately 'The LORD said to Samuel, "This is the one – anoint him!"' (1 Sam. 16:13). As the oil dripped from David's hair to the ground, his long career towards leadership began.

NATURE AND NURTURE

Josephus, the Jewish historian, said that Samuel whispered in his ear that God had chosen him to be king. It seems likely that this was the first intimation that David had of the unusual destiny that awaited him. Why did God choose David over his brothers? As the seven sons of Jesse passed before Samuel, their height and fine appearance masked the tangled and complicated family relationships which had formed their characters. Jesse belonged to a high-ranking clan of the Ephrathites in the tribe of Judah. His great-grandfather Boaz, the wealthy landowner, had married Ruth who was not from Israel but from Moab, a traditional enemy. With his first wife, Jesse had raised a family of seven sons, at least three of whom followed Saul into the army. Late in his life Jesse had married again the widow of one Nahash, about whom we know only his name. She brought with her two remarkable daughters, Zeruiah and Abigail. Of this second union David was born and grew up with Abishai and Joab, the sons of his step sister Zeruiah and Asahel and Amasa, the sons of Abigail.

He had an aging father who paid him little attention and seven older step brothers who seemed to dislike him. He also had two enterprising older step sisters and their families to contend with. David could have become an aggressive delinquent with a constant chip on his shoulder, used to fighting for whatever he could get and defiant of authority. But he did not because his heart was right. Samuel had told Saul earlier that 'the LORD will find the kind of man he wants (1 Sam. 13:14). Now Samuel had found him in the most unlikely circumstances. He was not found in the equivalent in that day of a happy nuclear family with two healthy, well-adjusted children attending the right schools and living in the best neighbourhood. He was the youngest in a widely extended family of children of different mothers, an aged father and all the domestic infighting that goes with that. In spite of his family background, David did his shepherd tasks with diligence and courage. Now David learns he is to be king over Israel.

HANDLING AMBITION

How do you handle information like this in your teens? Do you believe it? Do you take it seriously? There was no precedent for things like this happening, unless the rather recent random selection of Saul to be king was a precedent. One thing is clear from the sequel. He did not rush at the prospect. He took it slowly, gradually, in a principled fashion. That in itself is unusual. How did he manage to keep his ambition in check? The only clue we have in the text is, 'Immediately the spirit of the LORD took control of David and was with him from that day on' (1 Sam. 16:13).

There are strands in the Psalms, however, that may help us. In his poetry he makes some allusions to his early life. There was the influence of his mother. We do not know her name or where she came from. She had grown daughters that she took with her into her second marriage. David must have been a much longed-for son born in her later years. We do not know how long she lived. She was still alive when he had to flee, with all his family, as an outlaw, to the cave of Adullam, near the border with the Philistines, their enemy. After he saw to their safety from there, we hear no more of either parent. We know that he remembered and admired and tried to emulate the way his mother had served the LORD (Ps. 86:16; 116:16).

More than once he speaks with some awe of his birth. Are we hearing here a reflection of his mother's talk to her son in a not too welcoming household? Speaking about God, he said, 'It was you who brought me safely through birth, and when I was a baby, you kept me safe. I have relied on you since the day I was born, and you have always been my God' (Ps. 22:9-10). 'You created every part of me; you put me together in my mother's womb. I praise you because you are to be feared; all you do is strange and wonderful. I know it with all my heart. When my bones were being formed, carefully put together in my mother's womb, when I was growing there in secret, you knew that I was there – you saw me before I was born. The days allotted to me had all been recorded in your book, before any of them ever began' (Ps. 139:13-16). Whatever the source of such reflection, there is a strong sense of a divine providence shaping his life from the beginning.

He was conscious of being taught by God from early in his life (Ps. 71:17). There can be little doubt that a knowledge of the Law of Moses was a major part of this, although how he accessed that knowledge is obscure (Ps. 19:7-14).

Most of all, however, is the sense of security he had from knowing God. Psalm 23 is the best known of the Psalms. Every time we sing it we are trying to appropriate to ourselves the sentiments of a very secure young man. Having the LORD as his shepherd, he has everything he needs. All his physical and spiritual requirements are provided by God. Nothing makes him afraid, not even death. He is confident that his whole life will be taken care of. He trusted God from when he was young (Ps. 71:5).

Paul, the Christian apostle, was a great admirer of David. He said to another young man, 'godliness with contentment is great gain' (1 Tim. 6:6 NIV); perhaps that was the antidote to ambition.

TODAY'S CHALLENGES:

Being willing to do seemingly irrelevant jobs.
Making the transfer from hobby to service.
Assessing charisma.
Avoiding being stubborn.

'Whoever is faithful in small matters
will be faithful in large ones...'
(Luke 16:10)

2

Welcome to the Palace!

1 Samuel 16:14-23

WHAT NEXT?

'What next?' must have been David's question after Samuel whispered in his ear that he was destined to be king of Israel. The next thing was for him to be introduced to the person who most stood in the way of his dream being fulfilled. He went back a somewhat different person. The Spirit of the LORD took control of him from that day on (1 Sam. 16:13). He had greater confidence. He moved more decisively.

SUMMONED TO THE PALACE

In time, the summons came. His father called him in and said he was to go to the palace on the orders of the King. Jesse put together some gifts for the King, a goat, a donkey loaded with bread, a leather bag full of wine; and, 'by the way, don't forget your harp!' 'Harp? What will I need my harp for in the palace?' 'You will find out when you get there' (1 Sam. 16:19-20). David knew he was a good musician, but what had that to do with becoming king? He soon found out.

When he arrived at the royal compound, people there apparently knew him and were expecting him. 'Have you brought your harp?' was the first question. 'Yes, I have, but what is it needed for?' Then he was told. Saul, the king, was having moods in which he was dreadfully tormented by something. The explanation was that an evil spirit from the LORD was tormenting him. They were quite open about it and had actually talked to the king in those terms. They went on to suggest to the king that they look for a man who knew how to play the harp. Then when the evil spirit came on him, the man could play his harp, and he would be all right again. That was why Saul had sent for David. So they settled David into the palace and told him to stand by.

In time, one of his moods gripped Saul and they brought David in to play his harp. It worked! Saul got relief each time and, understandably, developed a fondness for David. As a cover for his real role as the royal comforter, they made him Saul's armour bearer. That was as near as he got to weapons and fighting.

MUSICAL INTELLIGENCE

It was a strange situation for David. What had been his hobby became his work. It did not seem to phase him. He did what was asked, even if it was far from what he had expected and far beneath someone who had secret royal pretensions. He was proving faithful in a little thing. In God's scheme of things that was the right preparation for greater responsibility (Luke 16:10).

Until then David had used the songs and his harp to help him deal with his own fluctuating moods out in the wilds with his sheep, and at the heart of his dysfunctional family. He continued to do this for the rest of his life.

Now he discovered that his singing and playing could be beneficial to the king when he was upset. The story flows flawlessly and obscures what became clear later on. In today's terms, David had multiple intelligences to fit him for his task as king. To a remarkable degree he had musical intelligence. He had a well developed right brain. He could play the harp, compose and sing songs to move the public on significant occasions, invent new instruments, and organise massive musical programmes for the Temple that was to be built after his death.

For the moment, however, his music brought him face to face with a significant feature in the personality of leaders. Ostensibly they controlled their country, but who or what controlled them? David's music therapy did not always work. Indeed, it did not work for long. In fact it began to have the opposite effect. After David's military prowess had been almost accidentally demonstrated and was being widely recognized, Saul fell into one of his moods again. He was raving like a madman. David came in and played his harp as before. This time it drove Saul to violence and he hurled a spear to kill his therapist. David managed to dodge the weapon and escape. It happened again later with the same result (1 Sam. 18:10; 19:9). The therapy was over and Saul's relationship with David went from bad to worse for the rest of Saul's life.

LEADERS AND CHARISMA

The foul moods of Saul are attributed by the historian to 'an evil spirit from the LORD'. This is contrasted with earlier statements that 'the spirit of the LORD took control of Saul' with good results (1 Sam. 10:6; 11:6). The writer also says, 'the spirit of the LORD took control of David from then on'. This seems to be this writer's way of saying that there is a special relationship between God and rulers. This is a general understanding throughout the Bible and it underlines that they get special help and are especially accountable to him.

There is another strange twist in Saul's spiritual experience. When the Spirit first took control of him, it was in the company of ecstatic prophets. 'Suddenly the spirit of God took control of him, and he joined in their ecstatic dancing and shouting. People who had known him before saw him doing this and asked one another, "What has happened to the son of Kish? Has Saul become a prophet?"

(1 Sam. 10:10,11) On this occasion this ecstatic experience resulted in him becoming a new and better person – for awhile. The quip, 'Has Saul become a prophet?' was meant to be a compliment.

Oddly enough, Saul had a second ecstatic episode much later on. He was searching for David in anger to kill him. He met a group of prophets singing and dancing. 'As he approached, the Spirit of God took control of him also, and he danced and shouted all the way to Naioth. He took off his clothes and danced and shouted in Samuel's presence, and lay naked all that day and all that night.' This is how the saying originated, 'Has even Saul become a prophet?' (1 Sam. 19:23-24). Saul apparently was of a temperament that was susceptible to ecstatic experiences. This time, however, there was no beneficial result in his behaviour or character. He got up, put on his clothes and continued to hunt down David who had done him no harm. The saying, 'Has even Saul become a prophet?' was no longer a tentative compliment. It was a cynical remark prompted by his obvious instability.

Ecstatic experiences in themselves bring no necessary moral change in a person. They are as open to evil as to good, and certainly they do not carry with them any stamp of God's approval although some think they do. Charisma is no justification for anything. The moral quality of a person and his acts has to be judged on different grounds. Saul's stubborn character was more significant than his charisma.

An earlier instance of this is the King of Egypt who persisted in his stubbornness and refused to let Israel go. The writer says clearly that the progression was from Pharaoh being stubborn to the LORD making Pharaoh incorrigibly stubborn with disastrous results for him and his people. Later, the Babylonian and Persian emperors went through the same syndrome.

DETERIORATION IN LEADERS

David became the victim of Saul's unstoppable deterioration, brought about by his presumption, stubbornness, disobedience and denial in all of this (1 Sam. 13, 14, 15). This was the only role model of a king available to David and had he followed this example the results would have been disastrous. Amazingly, he seemed to see that he was experiencing something he needed to steer clear of if he was to be a good leader.

Stubbornness in leaders is not an unusual phenomenon and often it precedes major departures in history. The Madness of King George III led to the loss of Britain's American colonies and marked the beginning of the rise of the USA to become the greatest power in the world. The intransigence of Slobodan Milosevich led to the dismemberment of Yugoslavia and the violent reshaping of the Balkans. The defiance of Saddam Hussein has led to changing the face of the Middle East.

This, however, is not the exclusive province of rulers of nations. Stubbornness in any leaders should be an occasion for them and those they lead to ask what is controlling them. David's patience and loyalty in the face of this stubbornness were the factors that led to the days of the tyrant being numbered. As they say, 'Blessed are the flexible, for they shall not be broken'.

But we are anticipating!

TODAY'S CHALLENGES:

Dealing with ulterior motives.
Questioning the standard approach to problems.
Seeing our battles from God's point of view.
Communicating clear goals to friends and enemies.

'Let no one despise your youth...'
(1 Tim. 4:12)

3
Just a Boy!

1 Samuel 17

The story of David and Goliath introduces us to the Philistines, the main military and political obstacle to the fulfilment of David's dream. There are no dates or ages in the story, but there is a definite emphasis on how young David was. The writer points him out as the youngest son in a large family. His father makes him the message boy taking food to his older brothers at the war. His oldest brother calls him 'a cheeky brat.' The king suggests he could not fight Goliath because he was 'just a boy.' Goliath, when he got a good look at David, was filled with scorn for him because he was just a nice, good-looking boy (1 Sam. 17:14, 17, 28, 42). He was probably in his mid-to-late teens and this is probably the key to what happened that day.

A DEPRESSED ARMY

The story, at first, has a weary, old and stale feel to it. For nearly six weeks there had been a daily charade enacted. Every morning, the Israelite and the Philistine armies marched out of their camps and formed up in battle order on the opposite slopes of a valley. Goliath, from the city of Gath, came out from the Philistine camp to challenge the Israelites. He stood over 9 feet tall, bronze helmet on his head, bronze greaves on his legs, a bronze coat of armour weighing 125 pounds protecting his body, and a bronze javelin slung on his back. His spear shaft looked like the bar on a weaver's loom and the iron point alone weighed 15 pounds. He was the champion of the Philistines, and towered above the Philistine rank and file at his back. He stood and shouted at the Israelites, 'What are you doing there, lined up for battle? I am a Philistine, you slaves of Saul! Choose one of your men to fight me. If he wins and kills me, we will be your slaves; but if I win and kill him, you will be our slaves. Here and now I challenge the Israelite army. I dare you to pick someone to fight me!'

The Israelites were terrified and made no response. There was no movement. It was stalemate. The Philistines did not attack. The Israelites were not called on to defend. It was a strange kind of warfare and the shots were being called by this giant of a leader from Gath.

It is worth asking how this Goliath became the leader of the Philistine army. Although his size was exceptional his leadership profile is not uncommon. Modern medical science might postulate that because of hyperactivity in his pituitary glands during adolescence his longitudinal bone growth had continued long beyond its normal cessation. Due to this genetic accident he had aggressively challenged, fought, and probably bullied his way to the top in his city. Everything rested on his greater reach with a sword and his longer throw with the spear. Now, with bravado and bombast he had hypnotized the Israelites and the Philistines into believing that the outcome of the battle depended on his physical size and strength alone. Mesmerized by his spectacular physique, both armies forgot about what really wins battles – strategy and tactics; the logistics of terrain and weaponry, the morale, fitness and the number of soldiers.

So there was no fighting. It was just stalemate creating a daily increasing supply problem to feed two armies while they waited each other out. The history also accounted for the spineless response of the Israelites. As often as not, the Philistines had beaten them in war, dominated their lives, made hope scarce and generally spread pessimism around.

A DIFFERENT WAY OF SEEING

All this changed when the boy came over the horizon and ran into the set piece battle lines. Everything now began to be seen through his youthful eyes. What first got David's attention, however, was the reward that Saul was offering to the Israelite who would take up the challenge and defeat this giant. 'King Saul has promised to give a big reward to the man who kills him; the king will also give him his daughter to marry and will not require his father's family to pay taxes.' These were attractive offers. Money was scarce in the chaotic conditions of life constantly threatened by raids from the Philistines. A financial reward and freedom from taxes for his father would make life a whole lot easier for all of them. We have to assume that David knew the king's daughter from his visits to Saul's palace and was not unattracted. Could the way to the throne be by becoming the king's son-in-law? That was a big temptation for a young man, especially a young man whose life was beginning to be controlled by the Spirit of God and who had ideas of himself being king one day.

David went around asking different soldiers, 'What will the man get who kills this Philistine and frees Israel from this disgrace? After all, who is this heathen Philistine to defy the armies of the living God?' He always got the same answer, but seems to have created something of a stir that brought a rebuke from his older brother and started a rumour that reached the King. It really was quite a spontaneous approach. It showed that he was not immune from the attractions of the reward for himself and his family and yet linked that to his deeper concern about what this whole episode was doing to the God of Israel. Whatever of these was his major concern, it fed the gossip that made the king send for him.

The contrasts between young David and old Saul in this encounter are striking. David had seen Saul in his worst moods and was learning to read him like a book, so he had an advantage. Behind the public façade, there was a sapping of confidence in Saul. So, he was scared by Goliath (1 Sam. 17:11). David's first words to Saul were, 'Your Majesty, no one should be afraid of this Philistine!' and he offered to go and fight him (1 Sam. 17:32). Behind the bravado, however, David saw how fragile Goliath's position was. The clanking of the bronze armour, the rippling muscles of his bare arms and the taunting challenge impressed and awed the opposition, but Goliath and the Philistines had all their strength in one area to the neglect of the others.

THE GOD FACTOR

David was marked out from everyone else that day by refusing to be deceived about the real issue: 'who is this heathen Philistine to defy the army of the living God?' (1 Sam. 17:26). Presented with the boastful posturing of Goliath and the demoralization of Saul's army, he saw where the real issue lay. The real problem was not as Chairman Mao would have said, in the objective conditions created by the size of one man, but in the subjective conditions that existed in the attitudes of the Israelites. They had lost faith in the promises that God had given to them as a nation. That was the real trouble. David saw the same scene as everyone else did, but saw it differently. He refused to be hypnotized by the popular view and penetrated to the one important factor that could be changed and that would change everything else: faith in God.

Saul's faith was at a low ebb. His relationship with God was under a cloud. The most he could muster was a weak and formal, 'Go, and the LORD be with you!' (1 Sam. 17:37). David was full of faith and very articulate about it. His private experience of God in as insignificant a place as the hills where he herded his father's sheep was the well from which he drank when confronted with a possible national disaster. Saul saw the army as his soldiers. To David, they were 'the armies of the living God' even when he had just entered their ranks on that day (1 Sam. 17:26). His faith showed most when he confronted Goliath between the two armies.

DRAWING ON LIMITED EXPERIENCE

David also drew from his previous experience. He told Saul, 'I take care of my father's sheep. Whenever a lion or a bear carries off a lamb, I go after it, attack it, and rescue the lamb. And if the lion or bear turns on me, I grab it by the throat and beat it to death. I have killed lions and bears, and I will do the same to this heathen Philistine, who has defied the army of the living God. The LORD has saved me from lions and bears; he will save me from this Philistine' (1 Sam. 17:34-37).

Experience does not by itself produce wisdom or ensure success, but experience interpreted accurately can. David recalled his own previous experiences of fear and danger and God's protection, and he projected accurately the lines of known past experience into a new situation, believing that God remains the same even if conditions change. If God protected him against lions and bears, he would also protect him against Goliath. If God helped him to save his flock, he would also help him to save his nation as long as he was doing what God wanted him to do. 'Give yourself to the LORD;' David wrote later, 'trust in him, and he will help you; he will make your righteousness shine like the noonday sun' (Ps. 37:5-6).

In choosing to defy Goliath and to trust in God's protection, David was not simply tackling the spectacular or tempting providence. He was not accustomed to fighting unnecessary battles. His objective was not to kill lions, it was to save sheep. He was not a hunter but a shepherd. He concentrated on protecting the sheep, not on building his own ego by slaying predators. When he accepted Goliath's challenge, David was motivated not only by the wealth, freedom from taxation, and marriage to the King's daughter promised by Saul, but by his desire to defend God's honour: 'This very day... I will give the bodies of the Philistine soldiers to the birds and animals to eat. Then the whole world will know that Israel has a God' (1 Sam. 17:46).

David also had the courage that Saul lacked to think independently outside the box. He was not encouraged by others in this action. Everyone, even King Saul, advised against what he proposed (1 Sam. 17:33). He had to back his own judgment. He had to ignore the opinions of lesser men and the taunts of his eldest brother, who questioned his motives and accused him of deserting his sheep to watch the excitement of the battle (1 Sam. 17:28).

Sticking to What He Knew

When Saul saw that David was determined to fight Goliath, he tried to tell him how to do it. He dressed David in a bronze helmet and a coat of armour and even gave David his own sword. This was a princely gift since at one point Saul and Jonathan had the only swords in the entire Israelite army. The Philistines held a monopoly on the iron trade and saw to it that no swords or spears were manufactured for Israel (1 Sam. 13:19-22). As David struggled to get into Saul's weighty armour it dawned on him it could be a handicap instead of an advantage. It made soldiers less likely to be wounded, but it also made them less mobile. On the other hand, his sling meant he could fight without getting within reach of the giant's sword or even the range of his great spear. In his bragging, Goliath has to invite David to 'Come on' and he would show him what he could do to him. David was not for coming on. He stayed back.

So, David rejected Saul's well-intentioned help. He insisted on staying within the field of his proven experience and competence. He shed Saul's heavy armour and armed himself only with his sling and stones. It changed the dynamic of the scene. Saul was stuck in the conventional approach to war, thinking that it depended on armour and skilled hand-to-hand fighting. David saw the advantage of fighting at a distance with a sling that would keep him out of range of all the advantages of height, strength and heavy armour on which the giant was relying. It was not that he had no use for conventional weapons. After stunning Goliath with the stone, David used a sword, Goliath's own sword, to kill him and cut off his head. Later, in fact, he added the sword to his own armoury (1 Sam. 21:9).

WHAT A LEADER SAYS

Saul had left the daily challenge of Goliath hanging in the air unanswered for six weeks. David was known as 'an able speaker' (1 Sam. 16:18). When he found himself out there between the armies, Goliath made a contemptuous little speech addressed to him. David, however, had things to say that would give meaning to what was to follow. He was not out to display his own personal prowess. He raised his voice and in the hearing of both armies he said, 'You are coming against me with sword, spear, and javelin, but I come against you in the name of the LORD Almighty, the God of the Israelite armies, which you have defied. This very day the LORD will put you in my power; I will defeat you and cut off your head. And I will give the bodies of the Philistine soldiers to the birds and animals to eat. Then the whole world will know that Israel has a God, and everyone here will see that the LORD does not need swords or spears to save his people. He is victorious in battle, and he will put all of you in our power.'

The speech was as important as killing Goliath. It gave it a context for both the Israelites and the Philistines. It explained the significance of what was happening. It identified that the motivation of David was not personal but national, not ambition but devotion to God.

Howard Gardner, the Harvard Educational Psychologist, analysed the leadership of twelve of the leaders in World War II and highlighted the importance of their speaking ability. 'While the majority of the leaders were creditable writers, by and large they were distinguished by their skill at spoken language. They bring to mind President Woodrow Wilson's testimony: "I have a strong instinct of leadership, an unmistakably oratorical temperament. My feeling has been that such literary talents as I have are secondary to my equipment for other things, that my power to write was meant to be a handmaiden to my power to speak and to organize actions." Indeed, if there is a single domain that each can be said to have mastered, it is the domain of public speaking. Speaking directly and convincingly to their various audiences. Roosevelt, Churchill, and de Gaulle were all masters of their nations' respective tongues, and all remain much quoted even decades after their death. Mussolini was a dramatic speaker graced by a beautiful voice and impressive theatrical gestures. Mao could electrify a crowd with his vivid images, while Lenin's fiery speeches played a notable role in the launching of the Russian Revolution. Indeed, of the various leaders surveyed here, only Stalin seems not to have been an outstanding speaker on the whole, although his speech to the Soviet people after the surprise Nazi invasion is credited with mobilizing patriotism and helping to ensure Germany's ultimate defeat. Hitler was the most amazing orator of the era.'[1]

The right brain of David was again in evidence in his ability to articulate publicly the issues that were being confronted on that day. It was a significant day for David. It brought him to public attention in a big way, but more significantly it showed in him qualities that were to be projected much further in future. It gave him more experience to convert into wisdom, and further strengthened his greatest assets, his faith in God and his desire to honour him.

1. Howard Gardner, *Leading Minds*' (BasicBooks, 1995), pp. 260-261.

TODAY'S CHALLENGES:

Reacting to a rival.
Dealing with envy.
Appointing people more able than yourself.

Paul said, 'always considering others
better than yourselves.'
(Phil. 2:3)

4

A Neighbour of Yours Who Is Better than You

1 Samuel 18–20

When the prophet Samuel told King Saul that God had rejected him, he said, 'Today the LORD has torn the kingdom of Israel from you and given it to a neighbour of yours who is better than you' (1 Sam. 15:28 JB).

To this man who was head and shoulders taller than anyone else that might have seemed an empty threat. Nothing happened immediately. Then when the Philistines attacked again, did he think that Goliath might match Samuel's prophecy? Goliath was even taller than Saul. Anyway, even if he saw Goliath as a threat to his position, it disappeared when David cut off Goliath's head. With great gusto, Saul and his army pursued the Philistine army all the way to the coast cities, killing and looting to their hearts' content.

RIVALRY BEGAN WITH A SONG

As they were returning back home, 'women from every town in Israel came out to meet King Saul. They were singing joyful songs, dancing, and playing tambourines and lyres. In their celebration the women sang, "Saul has killed thousands, but David tens of thousands."

Saul did not like this, and he became very angry. He said, "For David they claim tens of thousands, but only thousands for me. They will be making him king next!" And so he was jealous and suspicious of David from that day on. David, singing with his harp, had up to that point been effective in driving the evil spirit away. The praise songs of the women turned that around. The harpist, the armour bearer and the soldier suddenly was seen as a rival.

Rivalry comes naturally to people. It can be a good thing, bringing out the best in each person so long as they get on well. Mostly, however, it becomes unhealthy and damaging as it did here. In families, sibling rivalry can foster life-long competition and strife. Even sons see their fathers as rivals for the affection of their mothers. Girls can view their mothers in the same way. So Freud was provided with his Oedipus and Electra complexes.

History is littered with rivals like King John and Richard the Lion Heart in England in the twelth century. It was John's intransigence that led to the barons getting him to sign the Magna Carta.

Stalin and Trotsky became inveterate rivals. Trotsky wanted communism to develop internationally at the same time. Stalin wanted to create one communist state – Russia. Stalin prevailed. Trotsky had to leave Russia. It ended with Stalin having Trotsky assassinated in Mexico. World history might have been very different if the rival Trotsky had triumphed.

In Britain, rivalry has scarred the political landscape, whether it was the Tories with Edward Heath and Margaret Thatcher or Labour's Tony Blair and Gordon Brown.

And of course there are office politics in business, the public services and industry. Institutions like the army and the churches and the judiciary are not immune. Readers will have their own experience of rivalries that have spoiled their lives.

David was introduced to the shadow land of rivalry right at the beginning of his apprenticeship for kingship. Saul 'was jealous and suspicious of David from that day on' (1 Sam. 18:9).

BITTER PILLS TO SWALLOW

Even though David had acted naturally and innocently, he could hardly have made it worse for Saul if he had tried. His victory over Goliath galled the King. Saul belonged to the tribe of Benjamin, a tribe famous for its skill with the sling (Judg. 20:15-16). Saul must have felt very foolish after all his fuss, trying to get David to use his precious metal armour, only to watch David bring down Goliath with the very skill in which Benjaminites were supposed to excel. When he inquired whose son David was, and was reminded that he came from Bethlehem of Judah, a rival tribe, largest in numbers and richest in territory, it only made matters worse.

David's triumph over Goliath captured the imagination of the people, who went wild with delight over this young hero. Saul rewarded David with a high position in the army, and the officers and soldiers took the new commander to their hearts (1 Sam.18:6-8). '[E]veryone in Israel and Judah loved David because he was such a successful leader. Even Saul's own family started falling for the new hero. His son and heir to the throne, Jonathan, became David's bosom friend and swore a covenant of friendship with him (1 Sam. 18:1-4). The princess, his daughter Michal, made matters worse by falling in love with David, and he soon found that he had David for a son-in-law as well as a rival (1 Sam. 18:20-29). The old prophet Samuel, who had refused even to see Saul any more, protected David from Saul's messengers (1 Sam. 19:18-19).

Saul could only see the tapestry of his life's work unravelling. For centuries Israel had been a collection of tribes with no cohesion. At first Samuel, then Saul, had begun to weave them together, to create some unity, with leadership from Benjamin. God had been with Saul. Now, however, God had rejected Saul, who judged that David was in danger of creating an alternative centre of power and popularity. Soon he would rival even Saul's position on the throne. Because Saul was a small man, and getting smaller, he could not see that together they could have united all Israel. Instead, by his jealousy he divided the nation and brought about its further defeat.

THE PROGRESS OF RIVALRY

The progression of a rivalry that goes sour was detailed here perhaps more than anywhere else. This is how 1 Samuel 18 describes it.

- Anger (8)
- Jealousy (9)
- Suspicion (9)
- Raving (10)
- Violence (11)
- Fear (12)
- Entrapment (17, 20)
- Double-crossing (18-19)
- Enemy for life (29)

Saul's first reaction was anger when he heard the women's song: 'For David they claim tens of thousands, but only thousands for me. They will be making him king next!' (1 Sam. 18:8). Anger provoked suspicion, and Saul placed David under surveillance, jealously watching his movements. Every new report of David's success provided evidence that God was with David and had abandoned Saul, and Saul became afraid 'because the LORD was with David', afraid because David was successful, afraid because his daughter loved David. Soon his obsessive fear turned to violence. Twice he personally tried to kill David with a spear in the palace while he played his harp. Only his fleetness of foot saved David as he dodged the missile and escaped even as Saul pulled the quivering spear from the wall to hurl it again (1 Sam. 18:10-11, 29; 19:9-10).

When it became obvious that he could not personally catch David off guard, Saul resorted to more sophisticated means to do away with him. Pretending to honour him but secretly hoping that he would be killed, Saul promoted David, made him a commander of a thousand men and sent him on dangerous military missions. Instead, David's success in battle simply increased his popularity (1 Sam. 18:1-14).

Saul persisted in his duplicity. Remembering his promise to marry his daughter to the man who killed Goliath, Saul offered David his oldest daughter Merab: 'Here is my elder daughter Merab. I will give her to you as your wife on condition that you serve me as a brave and loyal soldier, and fight the LORD's battles' (1 Sam. 18:17). Saul was thinking that in this way the Philistines would kill David, and he would not have to do it himself. David's modest refusal foiled that scheme, but Saul tried again. When he discovered that his daughter Michal was in love with David, he was pleased. 'I'll give Michal to David; I will use her to trap him, and he will be killed by the Philistines' (1 Sam. 18:21). This time he tried to ensure David's death by asking a bride price of 100 Philistine foreskins. Undaunted, David undertook the bloody escapade, and, unscathed, he doubled the dowry, delivering to Saul 200 Philistine foreskins. Nothing seemed to touch David, and Saul became even more afraid.

Nothing deterred Saul from his mad programme of assassination by proxy, not even his own children's happiness. He had not scrupled to trade his daughters' happiness in marriage as the price for David's death. Now he sent messengers to kill David in his marriage-bed and roundly condemned his daughter for not co-operating in the plot and for allowing David to escape (1 Sam. 19:11-17). And when Jonathan would not betray David, obsessive rage possessed Saul and he hurled his spear at his son and heir, trying to kill him just as he had tried before to kill David (1 Sam. 20:33).

At the beginning of his reign he had been known for his ability to enlist able men. Wherever he found a man who was strong or brave, he would take him in his service (1 Sam. 14:52). At the end of his reign he could not tolerate David's ability or success anywhere near him. Ironically, his own regime weakened by the day because of his preoccupation with his rival. He could think only about David, constantly comparing David's present success to his own past success. The plots and schemes to secure his own position diverted Saul from the business of leadership and prevented him from doing anything constructive. Insecure in himself and no longer depending on God, he could not tolerate a rival.

THE WAY TO HANDLE RIVALRY

If Saul's life is a notable case study in envy, David's is even more remarkably a case study of how to handle envy. Amazingly, all through this period when Saul vented on David his venom and spite, David moved with complete equanimity and remained positive in his attitudes. He played his harp for Saul (1 Sam. 18:10) and he completed successfully every mission assigned to him. David did not let all his successes go to his head. When the suggestion of marriage to the King's daughter arose, his simplicity won through: "'Who am I and what is my family that I should become the king's son-in-law?...'" "It's a great honour...too great for someone poor and insignificant like me" (1 Sam. 18:18, 23).

How did David achieve such success and remain so positive in the face of Saul's envy? Like a refrain throughout the text comes the statement, 'The LORD was with him' (1 Sam. 18:12, 14, 28). That was his secret. His future did not depend on his own efforts. God would protect him. Whatever fame he won was God's gift. In the Psalms, David wrote:

> Don't be worried on account of the wicked;
> don't be jealous of those who do wrong.
> They will soon disappear like grass that dries up;
> they will die like plants that wither.
> Trust in the LORD and do good;

> live in the land and be safe.
> Seek your happiness in the Lord,
> and he will give you your heart's desire.

He handled Saul's envy, then, by ignoring it, by patiently trusting God and by behaving quite naturally. The man who is eaten up with repaying evil for evil has no energy left for constructive work. If David had been sidetracked into countering Saul's envy, he would not have had the success that won his acceptance by the people and secured his fame. It is greatness in a leader when, like Saul in his early days, he can surround himself with people of talent and distinction and when, like David, envy cannot touch him. The secret of such equanimity is the knowledge that in the last analysis success is won neither by brain nor by brawn, but is given by God.

TODAY'S CHALLENGES:

To whom should you be loyal?
Are commitments binding?
Handling demotion.

> Jesus said, 'The second most important commandment is this:
> "Love your neighbour as you love yourself."'
> (Mark 12:31)

5

Loving Your Neighbour as Yourself

1 Samuel 18–20

'Love your neighbour as you love yourself' began as one of about thirty miscellaneous rules in the Old Testament book of Leviticus. They were roughly based on the Ten Commandments. The 'neighbour rule' did not come to prominence, however, for a thousand years or more. When Jesus said it was the second most important commandment, it was included in three of the Gospels and reiterated by Paul (Rom. 13:9) in the New Testament. From there it has spread all over the world.

Oddly enough, there is only one person in the Bible who is actually said to have loved someone as he loved himself. It is Jonathan, son of Saul, and it was David that he loved (1 Sam. 18:1; 20:17). We have enough detail about the relationship to make it a case study of the subject, and it brings out several issues of public and private morality.

TWIN SOULS?

Plato was later to teach that at the creation all souls came from the Creator as twins. Separated by the imperfection of the world, each soul hungers and yearns and searches for its mate. Such an idea, though only a philosopher's fancy, almost seems confirmed in the case of David and Jonathan who, when they discovered each other, became one in spirit. As David talked, 'Saul's son Jonathan was deeply attracted to David and came to love him as much as he loved himself... Jonathan swore eternal friendship with David because of his deep affection for him. He took off the robe he was wearing and gave it to David, together with his armour and also his sword, bow, and belt' (1 Sam. 18:1-4).

It was a match! They were so alike! There was the same reckless daring. Jonathan with only his armour bearer took on a whole Philistine garrison without back-up and routed them. David single-handedly took on Goliath. They had the same faith. Jonathan told his young man, 'Maybe the LORD will help us; if he does, nothing can keep him from giving us the victory, no matter how few of us there are.' David stated his creed to Goliath, 'the LORD will put you in my power... the LORD does not need swords or spears to save his people. He is victorious in battle, and he will put all of you in our power' (1 Sam. 17:46-47). They were two of a kind. They took to each other at their first meeting. It was not just an inward feeling, although that was very strong. A bond was formed and immediately recognized by Jonathan with some very tangible tokens. It was as though he said to David, 'You will need more than a sling now!' and he gave him his own weapons when weapons were very scarce (1 Sam. 13:22). This, coming publicly from the crown prince, was no mean honour and it sealed the regular soldiers' enthusiasm for their new captain.

NEIGHBOUR LOVE IMPLIES LOYALTY

Their bond was soon tested. Saul's original enthusiasm for David waned and he started plotting against him. He sent David on dangerous military campaigns hoping he would not come back. He invented what seemed to be a frivolous exercise that was close to being a death sentence (1 Sam. 18:12-15, 20-29). All this was clandestine.

Then Saul came out into the open and told Jonathan and his officials that he planned to kill David. What was Jonathan to do? Should he defer to the king, his father, as everyone would expect? Should he just keep quiet and let things take their course? He did neither.

First, he was open and told David what he had learned and warned him to lie low. Then he stood up for David to his father. He became David's advocate and recited David's good qualities. He told the king that what he planned to do was wrong. David was not a threat. He was a valuable servant to whom Saul owed something. He alleged that Saul was being inconsistent and unreasonable. He won his father round and he vowed he would not kill David. David was reinstated to the court and to the army.

It did not last long. Saul was in the grip of something stronger than himself. His inner demons came back to haunt him right when David was playing his harp for the king. Saul gave an involuntary repeat performance of his attempt to pin David to the wall with his spear. His blood was up again. He was determined to finish David off. Only his daughter, Michal, prevented him from having David killed as he came out of his house one morning. When that failed he went after David in hot pursuit but failed again.

David went back to Jonathan for an explanation. It was a painful conversation. Jonathan had obviously been kept in the dark about what was going on. He tried to defend his father. David told him the truth. They made a plan for Jonathan to find out the lie of the land and report back. It got out of hand. When Jonathan spoke up for David again, Saul became abusive both of Jonathan and his mother. Violence flared up again and he even tried to kill Jonathan. Jonathan was mad and helped David to escape.

Loyalty is not a simple matter. What do you do when loyalty to a friend requires you to take sides against your family and particularly your father? In most cultures, family is the primary value. Honour your father and mother is not just one of the Jewish Ten Commandments. Kinship has been the most universal organising principle of society. It only began to be challenged in fifth-century Greece where your locality or your city became the primary value. That was the price of democracy becoming possible.

What do you do when loyalty to a friend requires you to speak against your king, your chief, your boss? In Jonathan's case, it was life-threatening to do so. It has often been so. Sometimes the issue is standing up for the truth. The dilemma is even greater when a stand has to be taken publicly as with Jonathan.

Jesus entered into the debate unequivocally when he said that if you love father and mother more than him, you could not be a disciple of his (Matt. 10:37).

PROMISE-KEEPING WITH NEIGHBOURS

It seems that from day one, the relationship between Jonathan and David was very consciously entered into. 'Jonathan swore eternal friendship with David because of his deep affection for him' (1 Sam. 18:3). The old language was, 'He made a covenant with David'. It was clearly a very self-conscious commitment by each man to the other.

When the break with Saul was looking like being inevitable, David was very anxious that their promises remain valid, even if they were to be physically separated. 'Please do me this favour, and keep the sacred promise you made to me.' Later, it is Jonathan's turn to plead when it looks as though there might be a danger to his own life: 'if I die, show the same kind of loyalty to my family for ever. And when the LORD has completely destroyed all your enemies, may our promise to each other still be unbroken. If it is broken, the LORD will punish you' (1 Sam. 20:16 GNB). Once again Jonathan made David promise to love him, for Jonathan loved David as much as he loved himself' (1 Sam. 20:14-17). He wanted David to extend his commitment to his family if he were to die. This was a hard thing to ask with Saul having become totally hostile to David. Yet there followed a very solemn renewal of their promise before the LORD that bound their families together. We know the outcome. Saul and Jonathan were killed in battle and David kept his promise to Jonathan both in respect of Saul while he lived and of Jonathan's children after father and son had both died.

Promise or covenant-keeping is the way the LORD wants to relate to us men and women. He has structured it differently in different phases of the sacred history. Finally, God committed himself to us by sending his son, Jesus, to live, die and rise again on our behalf to show us the extent of his love. He wants us voluntarily to commit ourselves to him and then stick with it. Our commitment to him carries with it the same commitment to our neighbours.

I sense two conflicting trends today. One is an ever-increasing reluctance to commit ourselves for any length of time to anyone or anything. The other is a hungering for the luxury of being able really to trust people because we know they make and keep their promises. This hunger for trust has been demonstrated in a remarkable way in the USA in the last fifteen years.

Bill McCartney was a well-known American Football coach. With some friends he began a men's movement in 1990 called 'Promise Keepers'. He sensed that men could help each other in a wholly male context in a way that was not so easy in mixed gender events. They worked out and made The Seven Promises of a Promise Keeper, covering their commitments to God, friends, purity, family, church, community and the world. They felt that these framed a life of Christian integrity.

They organised massive rallies in sports stadia in many states. In 1996, 1.2 million men met in 22 stadia conferences to strengthen each other. In 1997, an estimated one million men gathered from every race, nationality and most Christian denominations in the National Mall in Washington D.C. for a six-hour Prayer Event. The phenomenal growth of The Promise Keepers has to indicate a real hunger among men for more reliable relationships in families, churches, work places and society generally. There is little doubt that it revolutionized the lives of thousands of men.

In a sense Jonathan and David could have been the patron saints of the Promise Keepers for they were the originals. Loving our neighbour as ourselves must mean keeping promises to our neighbours as we would like them to make and keep promises to us.

I Will Be Second to You

The early divestment by Jonathan of his robe, belt, sword and shield and his gift of them to David, proved to be highly symbolic, if not prophetic. In their last secret meeting out in the wilderness it came out. 'Jonathan went to him there and encouraged him with assurances of God's protection, saying to him, "Don't be afraid. My father Saul won't be able to harm you. He knows very well that you are the one who will be the king of Israel and that I will be next in rank to you." [I" will be second to you – NIV"]. The two of them made a sacred promise of friendship to each other. David stayed at Horesh, and Jonathan went home.' Jonathan had come to a conclusion that David had known all along that David was destined to be king and successor to his Jonathan's father.

One can only imagine the effect on David of such a statement from Jonathan. It must have been a mixture of huge relief for himself and unbearable distress for his friend. They parted for the last time. David went back to his band of outlaws in the wilderness of Judea. Jonathan went back to the court of his father. Jonathan, in spite of his admission, did not join David's band. He remained loyal to his father and died by his side in battle. What a moral giant of a man! How did he show such magnanimity?

Charles Kingsley was once asked about the secret of his happy, buoyant spirit all through life. He answered, 'I had a friend.' Jonathan too had a friend, David. David and Jonathan, their names a byword for neighbours who loved each other as themselves, are inseparably linked wherever the Bible has been translated and read.

TODAY'S CHALLENGES:

Losing a job.
Becoming a refugee.
Are white lies justified?
Coping with fear and insecurity.
The effect of your actions on others.

So stand ready, with truth as a belt tight round your waist
(Eph. 6:14)

6

Living by His Wits

1 Samuel 20–22

David had a dream start to his public career. Repeated military successes, no failures; celebrity status in the country; marriage to the king's daughter who loved him; and best friends with the crown prince, Jonathan. He handled it all with amazing modesty, even humility, for a young man, hardly yet 20 years of age.

The dream died in two stages. The first was temporary when he narrowly escaped being killed by a spear that the king hurled at him when he was doing his minstrel duty. Jonathan talked his father out of his murderous intent. David was restored to the royal favour, service in the palace and on the battlefield.

Saul's demons returned and he turned against David again, permanently this time. It was now official. David was an outlaw and had to run for his life, without food or weapons. He was on his own. He was poor. He did not know where the next meal was coming from. His life was in constant danger. His friends dared not even to acknowledge him. He was separated from his young wife. She would be married to someone else.

CLEVER IMPROVISATION

He went five miles south to Nob, a settlement of priests. There had not been time for the word to get out that he was an outlaw, so David made up a story about being suddenly sent by Saul on a secret mission. He needed a weapon for himself, and food for his men when he would rendezvous with them at an unnamed site. Ahimelech, the priest, swallowed the deception and helped him out, but the incident was noticed by a hostile foreigner who happened to be there at the time. He was Doeg from Edom.

David moved quickly to put as many miles as he could between himself and the palace. He walked about thirty miles south-west in a panic. He got himself out of Israel and into the Philistine city of Gath, ruled by Achish, an enemy of Israel. As he went about Gath he discovered that they knew who he was. He had to get out of there, so he started acting like a madman. He must have been pretty convincing, for they ran him out of town. It was a very close shave.

Where could he go now? No town was safe either in Philistia or Israel. He slipped back into Judah about thirteen miles east of Gath and, among the foothills, discovered some habitable caves near the town of Adullam. He had to think. It was time for reflection. Popular culture believes that men deal with stress by retreating to their caves and by becoming more withdrawn. It was to a literal cave that David retreated to reflect on what had happened to him.

His fortunes had plummeted in a matter of weeks from being the Number One celebrity in the country to being and having absolutely nothing himself and posing a danger to everyone else. He had no prospects. As they say in Ghana, he had gone from grace to grass. How does a young man of David's age handle something like that, especially in the light of what the prophet Samuel had whispered to him about being king one day?

He started living by his wits, improvising, making up stories as he went. They say that in war the first casualty is truth. It would also seem to be the first casualty when you are on the run as a refugee. A second natural tendency is to start using other people – just to survive.

Abraham Maslow is known for his theory of a hierarchy of needs. People are motivated by unsatisfied needs in a certain order, and lower needs need to be satisfied before higher ones. They are:

- Physiological needs: air, food, water, sleep, sex, etc.
- Safety needs: security, stability, both physical and psychological.
- Love needs: belonging, acceptance.
- Esteem needs: self-esteem from achievement and attention and recognition from others.
- Self-actualisation: the desire to be everything that one is capable of becoming.

David had been dreaming about self-actualization ever since the anointing by Samuel. Now he was stripped of everything and he had to revert to the bottom of the list of needs and be concerned about food and safety – just to survive. He told fabricated stories and play-acted when he had to. It was not a pretty picture. But there was more to it than that.

THE OUTWARD AND THE INWARD

We have two parallel lives of David. There is the straightforward official biography embedded in the two books of Samuel. It gives the impression of being factual, reasonably chronological and objective. David is presented as very practical, matter of fact, outwardly in control and taking things in his stride. In addition we have glimpses of the inside emotional story in poems that he wrote that form part of the book of Psalms.

We all have such parallel lives, the outward and the inner. I learned this very forcefully when undergoing a test by a management guru. His set of questions were designed to flush out and make conscious these parallel lives. It was quite a revelation. Indeed it was quite a shock. It taught me that how a person behaves outwardly is no indication as to how they need to be treated. A person can look very confident on the outside and be a mass of insecurity underneath. People have internal needs and motives that can rarely be seen by others. Good managers find ways to get to know these internal needs in their teams and do what they can to see that they are met. They are not misled by the front that a person puts on. The performance of the person who feels understood is enhanced enormously. The histories show David's front. The Psalms reveal his inner self. Four psalms come from this period of David's life (34, 52, 56, 142).

In the narrative of David's escape from Saul he adapts effortlessly to each situation as it arrives and moves on. The underlying situation in the psalms he wrote is very different. He was ready to give up. He does not know what to do. He feels he is entirely on his own, no one to help, protect or care for him. He was sometimes sunk in despair or deeply distressed.

ENEMIES

The new reality for David was that he had enemies. The historical account marks the moment of transition, Saul 'was his enemy as long as he lived' (1 Sam. 18:29). David had at first tried not to believe this. Now there could be no doubt. His enemies were real and were to be part of the furniture of his life from then on. This is his complaint, 'My enemies persecute me all the time… [They] make trouble for me all day long; they are always planning how to hurt me!' (Ps. 56:1).

Perhaps the most dominant theme in the whole Book of Psalms is 'enemies'. The word occurs 156 times in the 150 psalms. It occurs in 42 of the 73 psalms traditionally attributed to David himself. At this time the main emotion that his enemies inspire in him is fear (Ps. 56:3, 4, 8, 11). We are not surprised that in the cave of Adullam he is battling with this fear.

Psalm 34 takes us into his mind and heart and lets us see the anatomy of this fear. It brought a sense of oppression (vv. 2, 5). He felt totally helpless and hopeless (vv. 6, 18) and shed tears (56:8). It did not help that he was sometimes hungry for lack of food and in danger of his very life (vv. 10, 17). As far as his dream of kingship was concerned, he was discouraged (v. 18). It was just trouble, trouble, trouble (vv. 6, 17, 19).

Battling Fear

As he paced around the caves in Adullam, he wrestled with these chaotic emotions and he comes out, not unscathed, but a wiser and a better man. Clearly he was overcome by the magnitude of his deliverance so many times. He could not believe he was still alive and he realized it was only because the LORD had stepped in to save him. He did not congratulate himself on his ingenuity in getting the food and weapon he needed from the priest with his fabricated story. He was not proud of the madman act that he put on to get driven out at least alive from Gath. It was rather the opposite. In Psalm 34 he seems ashamed of his lying. We can just hear him singing to those who came to him in the cave, 'Come, my young friends, and listen to me, and I will teach you to honour the LORD. Would you like to enjoy life? Do you want long life and happiness? Then hold back from speaking evil and from telling lies. Turn away from evil and do good; strive for peace with all your heart.' This enabled him to get the LORD back in his sights and his promises became real again (Ps. 56:10). He moved from, 'When I am afraid, I will trust', to 'I will trust and not be afraid.'

New Responsibility

Word got about that David was in the cave of Adullam. He did not remain alone in the hills for long. His leadership ability, his military reputation, his attractive poetic temperament, in short his charisma inevitably drew others to him. Charisma is that indefinable quality of leadership that attracts followers and inspires them to dedicate themselves to a cause, 'When his brothers and the rest of his family heard that he was there, they joined him'. They themselves fled from the unpredictable anger of Saul until David found them safe lodging in the neighbouring kingdom of Moab.

Under Saul, the country was being neglected or badly administered. The number of discontented citizens grew. People who were oppressed or in debt or dissatisfied flocked to David, about 400 men in all, and he became their leader. Some, no doubt, suffered from genuine oppression, unjust debts, or justifiable dissatisfaction. Others were probably parasites attracted by the free food and someone to take care of their needs. With this motley rabble David had to learn the hard way about leadership and mould a company of firm friends and well disciplined, able soldiers.

It was not an enviable way to start a political career. Not only did David have to defend himself against Saul; not only did he have to fight the Philistines; now he had to feed, clothe, train, and settle the disputes of 400 malcontents who looked to him for leadership.

THE BIRDS COME HOME TO ROOST

A priest named Abiathar arrived one day with a story David did not want to hear. He was the son of Ahimelech, the priest at Nob who had listened to David's fabricated story, believed his lies and gave him food and a sword. Recently, Saul had been complaining that his officers were not doing enough to locate David. He accused them of secretly favouring David. The hostile foreigner, Doeg, who had witnessed the priest Ahimelech helping David, spoke up and told his story. Saul sent for the priest and all his relatives. Saul accused Ahimelech of plotting with David against him. Ahimelech admitted what he had done and said it was out of respect and admiration of a man he had no reason to believe was not the most faithful servant Saul had. He denied plotting but it did no good.

Saul ordered him, all his eighty-five relatives, and all the people and livestock in the village to be slaughtered. The guards refused, but Doeg, the man from Edom, did what the King wanted and slaughtered them all except Abiathar. He alone escaped and brought the report to David in Adullam.

FALSEHOOD LEADS TO MASSACRE

David was mortified with guilt for he had some misgivings about Doeg at the time. He admitted, 'I am responsible for the death of all your relatives.' This was the collateral damage from his using false pretences to get Ahimelech to assist his flight from Saul. This was the consequence of the white lies he had told to save his skin. It is to his credit that he makes no excuses. He accepts responsibility for his actions.

None the less, he had no good opinion about the callous action of Doeg in reporting Ahimelech to curry favour with Saul and then, by his own hand, butchering a whole village. We get his assessment of Doeg in Psalm 52. It must have made David smart to write, 'here is a man who did not depend on God for safety, but... looked for security in being wicked' (Ps. 52:7). He knew that he himself had strayed for awhile into that kind of territory when he was living solely by his wits. The terrible massacre happened because he did so. At least in the cave of Adullam he came to his senses and shifted his attitude.

TODAY'S CHALLENGES:

Respect and care for parents.
Addiction to an irrecoverable past.
Taking advantage of friends.

'[T]he one thing I do, however, is to forget what is behind me
and do my best to reach what is ahead.'
(Phil. 3:13)

7

Dealing with the Past

1 Samuel 22:1-4; 2 Samuel 23:13-17

FAMILY AS A VALUE

David's parents, brothers, servants and farm hands had elected to come and cast their lot in with David, the youngest boy. It was not safe for them to stay on the farm at Bethlehem when Saul was ready to kill anyone who could even be suspected of siding with David.

Living in a cave with a motley and growing band of outlaws was no life for an old man and his aged wife. What should be done with them? The brothers and the rest of the household could stay on but some other plan seemed necessary for his elderly parents. David was one sixteenth part Moabite from his Moabite Great-grandmother on his father's side (Ruth 4:18-22). He decided to trade on that historic connection. He personally escorted his elderly mother and father seventy miles on foot or with a donkey, and sought asylum for them at the court of the King of Moab. They stayed there as long as David was hiding in the cave (1 Sam. 22:1-5).

This special care for his parents is very touching. It is the only reference to David's mother in the historical texts. David does speak of her with warmth in the Psalms (see chapter 1). His call from God, even if it was not yet altogether clear, was not allowed to supplant the respect and care he owed to his parents. This was a value in that society enshrined in the Ten Commandments.

Jesus pointed out that it was not uncommon for grown children to neglect and shut out their parents and give a religious excuse for doing so. He calls this gross hypocrisy and defiance of God's Law (Mark 7:9-13). In most of the world, probably for two-thirds of its population, care and respect for parents is a high value. The Qu'ran puts this as second only to obedience to God. Confucius, the Chinese philosopher, formalized it into almost an absolute requirement. He believed that if people could learn to perform their familial roles properly they would in turn be able to perform their roles in society and government properly (4:20, Analects). Hindus also put a high value on care for elderly parents.

Only in the West is this natural duty ignored. The West behaves as though it is the job of the state to provide pensions and care for the elderly, while their offspring get on with making money and pursuing happiness. Within the state, opposing parties compete with each other to trumpet the provisions they will make for the elderly. There is never a whisper, however, that the real need is for children to honour and provide for their parents. Do we want the rest of the world to become like us in devaluing the parental bond?

Yet, with Jesus, this duty is not unqualified. Jesus had his own differences with his parents (Luke 2:48-51; 14:26) and comes out emphatically against making family the primary value. He has to resist their attempts to control him. His disciples were not to love parents and family more than him. For a time his family disappears from the story. Yet on the cross, Jesus' care for his mother shines out from the depths of his own agony (John 19:26). After the resurrection his mother and brothers are back with the believers (Acts 1:14). It is a fine balance to get family and God in a proper perspective, yet we have to maintain it.

NOSTALGIA

Back in the foothills of Judah, David found that the Philistines were up
to their old tricks of raiding Israel. They had seized Bethlehem, David's
home town, at harvest time, no doubt to carry off the harvested crops
for themselves. This piled on the agony for David. He could not go
back home because Saul was after him. Even his family had to move
out and come to him for protection. Now, in addition, the Philistine
garrison was in Bethlehem and the possibility of returning there was
even more remote.

He felt homesick and weary of his fugitive life. He said wistfully,
'Oh that one would give me drink of the water of the well of
Bethlehem which is by the gate!' (2 Sam. 23:15 KJV). It was a natural
wish and full of understandable nostalgia. It was a wish that revealed
a set of values. He valued freedom of movement in his own country
without restriction. Bethlehem and home were places to which he
could not go because of the political situation, and it was natural that
he should long to be free to return.

He valued peace and respite from the hardships, dangers and
tragedy of war and political persecution. He was a hunted man and
not only had he to provide for himself, but also for these men who
made him their leader.

He valued the simple things of home. The well by the gate was
a place for meeting friends of both sexes, for local gossip and news,
for laughter and teasing with the older people indulgently looking on.
It spoke of the warmth of belonging and acceptance, so much a part
of home. It had memories of his parents and his brothers and sisters
and the good times they had together. He wished it could be again as
it had been, homely and happy.

He valued the regular supply of creature comforts. That well was
a symbol of provision, always to hand, of the necessities of life. The
water was there just for the taking, and everyone had enough, perhaps
not too much at times, but enough.

He expressed a whole set of values in the sentence, 'Oh that one would give me drink of the water the well of Bethlehem, which is by the gate!' We all know what it is to wish that the past could come back.

I WISH...

We all know how we would finish the sentence: How I wish that ... so and so was still alive; that my friend was not so far away; that I had my old job to go to; that I had the respect and status I used to enjoy; that things were simpler and more straightforward as they used to be; that people would work harder, be more reliable and more honest as they used to be.

GETTING THINGS IN PERSPECTIVE

Yet even before we go on with the story, it was not all great. His family had not been ideal. Read the earlier stories and you have the distinct impression that David was late in arriving in Jesse his father's family and was much resented by the others and not very well treated. We can be very selective in what we choose to remember and how we paint the past. We need to remember it all, the bad and the good.

David was quickly jolted out of his maudlin nostalgia. Three of his best and bravest men, whose names we do not know, heard him express his wish. Their attachment and devotion to him was so strong that they slipped away unnoticed to do something about his depression. They went stealthily and broke through the enemy lines, filled their water bottle at the well in Bethlehem and made the dangerous journey back without mishap, and presented their hero with his request (2 Sam. 23:16).

What an action that was! How much it said! It must have done much to restore David's flagging spirits to discover that he had men like that who without pay or a specific order took their lives in their hands and acted so bravely. Their names are not even known. They are just three of the thirty chief men. It does not say which.

A CHANGE OF VALUES

When David saw the water, he was dumbfounded. He had not meant to be taken seriously. He did not even know that his wish had been heard. When he saw that water bottle he was overcome with deep emotion. 'He poured it out to the LORD and said, "Far be it from me, O LORD, that I should do this. Shall I drink the blood of the men who went at the risk of their lives?"Therefore he would not drink it'.

He saw the water no longer as the clear, cool and fresh water he remembered, the symbol of all that meant home and peace and freedom and plenty. He saw it as crimson red, the symbol of lifeblood risked to bring it to him, and he would not drink it. There were two sides to his action.

He would not consume it selfishly, because of its cost. His nostalgia became almost criminal when he realized the risk it had brought to others whom he valued.

He poured it out to the LORD. He offered it as a libation, a drink offering to God. He made the occasion an act of worship. Perhaps these men who had brought it, felt at first, as they saw it soak into the ground, 'What a waste! Why did we bother?' A moment's reflection, however, assured them that a man who set such a value on their actions would never waste anything.

David, in that moment, realized that life had moved on. He could not go back. He should not go back. He did not go back. In fact the text does not show him ever going back to Bethlehem. This was the beginning of a greater exodus in his life. He had to leave behind, not just Bethlehem, but Judah, his tribe. His call was to greater things in all Israel. A hankering after childhood memories would not help him. He had to jettison what has been called his 'five-year-old world view'. He had to grow into his call. This meant a re-ranking of his values that did not put home and family and their associated preferences at the very top. The rest of his life is the story of how he tried to do this.

Jesus was confronted with similar challenges. He was also born in Bethlehem, but never went back. He was brought up a Jew, but he loved the whole world. He found it well-nigh impossible to get people to grasp what he was about. Perhaps the closest Jesus came to what David went through with the water from Bethlehem was when a woman brought a jar of hugely expensive perfume. She poured out the whole jar and used it like water to wash his feet and freshen up his hair. Jesus was staggered by her action and the love and insight it showed. He implied that by her action she demonstrated the very essence of what he and his gospel were about. This was in marked contrast to Judas and the other disciples.

He had set his face as a flint to leave Galilee and its familiar and more friendly surroundings and go to Jerusalem to face death at the hands of his enemies. Here was one person who had picked up the clues and understood what was happening. She was anointing him beforehand, for his burial! He was deeply gratified and went on, like David, to express appreciation and make the values statement, 'wherever the gospel is preached all over the world what she has done will be told in memory of her'.

But we are talking about David and the incident of the water demonstrated that his continued attachment to the things he used to like could be costly to others. He could no longer afford such indulgence. He had to grow up – and fast. He did, and he did it before God, making a drink offering of the water brought with such risks.

There is a child in all of us. Nothing can change that; but we sometimes take risks and put others at risk when we go on indulging our instincts unregulated in the light of reason or in the light of God. We certainly stunt our own growth as persons.

This was a problem in the early church at Corinth. They were listening to their childhood biases and ended up quarrelling with those they did not like or felt were not their kind of people (1 Cor. 3:1-4).

Jewish churches had another version of the same problem. Their Christian faith seems not to be much more than an add-on to what they had been as Jews before they believed in Jesus. If they had heard what they were taught, it did not seem to make any difference. They did nothing about integrating it into the way they behaved or looked at things. The result was that they made poor moral judgments and were not really good at distinguishing between good and evil. They needed to mature in their Christian understanding (Heb. 5:11-14).

Paul was like David when he said, 'when I became a man, I put away childish things'. This is a real test for leaders. Will they be driven by unquestioned instincts that have their root in nothing more than their own circumscribed childhood preferences? All our childhoods are inevitably circumscribed, some more than others. Will leaders have the courage and the will to face up to and understand their real selves and change where the greater good calls for change?

TAKING ADVANTAGE OF OTHERS

More than that, will leaders take the extra step of refusing to take advantage of the loyalty of their followers, as David unwittingly took advantage of his three heroes, and make their lives and their wellbeing their first consideration? And will they do this before God to whom they are ultimately accountable? Leaders are not really ready to face their task until they have exorcized the petty things within themselves that are nothing but a hangover from their childhood. This is complicated because these three heroes, by their actions, were endorsing David's whim as legitimate. They understood him because they were like him. They were the kind of people whom he attracted, and about forty of them are named as helping him to become king.

TODAY'S CHALLENGES:

Admitting our need of God.
Putting ourselves publicly on God's side.

> 'These people, says God, honour me with their words,
> but their heart is really far away from me.'
> (Mark 7:6)

8

A Power Greater than Himself

1 Samuel 23

No interpretation of David's career can ignore the fact that a great part of his success comes from his awareness of the spiritual dimension in life. There is no question about his military genius, his way with people and a whole battery of other remarkable gifts. But David would neither have been the man he was nor have built what he achieved if it had not been for this central dimension in his life. The Psalms provide the greatest evidence of how much he prayed, but the narrative also shows a man who believed that God was real and that God was God and he was involved in the affairs of men.

David's spirituality, however, fluctuated. Sometimes it went quiet and God did not seem to be in his thoughts at all. This was true in the period between his flight from Saul and when he found himself, scared out of his wits, in the cave of Adullam (see ch. 6). At other times it floods back strong and vital as in the incidents we consider here when the LORD is very much in his consciousness.

HE ASKS FOR DIRECTION

The town of Keilah was a Judean town that was just gathering in its harvest. The enemy Philistines sent out raiding parties to loot the threshing floors and carry off the grain. They were of David's tribe. Saul could have sent his army to offer protection, but he did not. Although David had no responsibility in the matter and although Saul was likely to misinterpret his intervention, David, the patriot, wanted to do something for his people. By the method of the day he asked the LORD if he should attack. The answer was 'Attack!' His men were not so sure. He asked for direction a second time and got the same answer (1 Sam. 23:1-5). David's men attacked and defeated the Philistines, captured their livestock, and relieved the town.

His very success, however, created two difficulties. It put the citizens of Keilah in the compromising position of appearing to be linked with David. This would do them no good with Saul. It also put David in a walled town where he would be very vulnerable if caught between the thumb of an outside attack and forefinger of a frightened citizenry. In fact, when Saul heard that David had gone to Keilah, he said, 'God has put him in my power. David has trapped himself by going into a walled town with fortified gates.' Saul immediately mobilized his troops to besiege Keilah and capture David and his men.

HE ASKS FOR INFORMATION

David was frustrated. With divine encouragement he had successfully attacked the Philistines and rescued Keilah, only to create more trouble for them and himself. With the memory of the massacre of the priests of Nob that he had caused still fresh in his mind, he prayed again. His need this time was for an intelligence report. Was Saul on his way, and if he was, would the people of Keilah hand him over? He had no time to send spies. He did, however, have Abiathar, the priest, the sole survivor of Saul's revenge at Nob. He had brought with him the ephod, the embroidered vestment worn by the priests when asking direction from God. Through Abiathar, David now consulted God again and learned that Saul would attack and that the people of Keilah would surrender him to Saul in spite of the help he had given them.

Now that he had the information, he had to make his own decision. Information is not direction. It just gives you a choice to act in one way or the other. David and his men, now numbering about 600, took to the hills. Eager to act for the welfare of people, but in difficulty with a system that crowded him out, David resorted to the God who controls men and events, and God helped him to escape.

HE ASKS FOR PROTECTION

People in the Desert of Ziph to which he escaped had the same attitude as the people of Keilah. They were on the side of Saul. They sent informers to court the king's favour and betrayed David's whereabouts to Saul: 'David is hiding in our territory at Horesh on Mount Hachilah, in the southern part of the Judaean wilderness. We know, Your Majesty, how much you want to capture him; so come to our territory, and we will make sure that you catch him' (1 Sam. 23:19-20). The situation David had feared inside Keilah began to be re-enacted even in the open countryside. Saul went after David. Saul and his men were on one side of the hill, separated from David and his men, who were on the other side. They were hurrying to get away from Saul and his men, who were closing in on them and were about to capture them. What could he do? Humanly speaking there was nothing to do but run, but for David there was still one way he could take. He could go to a power greater than himself. He could go to God, and he did. Psalm 54 records a prayer said to have been offered on this occasion.

He is very frank. 'Proud men are coming to attack me; cruel men are trying to kill me' (v. 3). What does he pray for? He prays to be saved (v. 1). He asks God to use their own evil to punish his enemies (v. 5).

Why does he think God will listen to him? He clearly has a personal sense of God's availability to help and defend him (v. 4) because God has done it before (v. 7). It is also clear that he was a worshipper of

God in the way of Israel, offering the sacrifices ordained by God in his covenant with his people (v. 6).

There is, however, a more subtle reason for his confidence. Those who are chasing him do not care about God (v. 3). He does care about God. He believes in God. He believes in a power greater than himself and thinks that it is important enough to be public about it. For him, belief and trust in God is not an optional extra which we may adopt or leave without it making any difference. God is there and he can be approached. So he approached him and it made a great difference.

A message arrived for Saul, "Come back at once! The Philistines are invading the country!" So Saul stopped pursuing David and went to fight the Philistines' (1 Sam. 23:27-28). David was saved again.

From this dramatic escape David learned that God has more ways than one of answering prayer. God defied human wisdom and enabled David without benefit of sword or shield to kill Goliath with a slingshot. Now he protected David without the defences of a walled city or stone fortress. In learning to consult God, David had become the realist who saw life as a whole and took into account all the factors. He had learned to acknowledge the spiritual dimension in all of life and to operate in conscious co-operation with, and dependence on, God.

THE GOD WHO IS THERE

David could not be neutral about God or about how people thought about him. It is Saul, the King, and his men he is describing when he says, 'Proud men are coming to attack me; cruel men are trying to kill me – men who do not care about God.' Now, Saul was not irreligious. In his earlier life there had been several marks of a modest and God-fearing person. After he became king serious deterioration set in. He retained the language of faith but by his behaviour denied the reality. He pursued and tried to kill David for no good reason. It is little wonder that he came to the conclusion that Saul and his men did not care much for God.

The God of Israel was the Creator of heaven and earth and everything in them. He fashioned people when they were still in the womb. In all of this he was just and good, faithful and reliable. So he was on the side of justice and goodness and opposed to their opposites. Those who were bad and unjust, deceitful and unreliable, could not possibly care for God. That gave David standards and he tried mostly to adhere to them.

David and Saul represent two different attitudes to religion in public life. Saul had the language, even publicly, but not the reality. David had both the language and the reality of private devotion, moral uprightness (mostly) and public commitment. Jesus drew the same distinction when he described the hypocritical Pharisees as those who honoured God with their words, but their heart was really far away from him (Mark 7:6).

Respect for authority.
Over-reading providence.
Not being stampeded by popular support.
Readiness to talk and confront.
Commitment to reconciliation.

Jesus, answered "You have authority over me
only because it was given to you by God.'"
(John 19:11)

9

Not a Rebel

1 Samuel 24

A LUCKY BREAK

Saul left David alone only for a short time. When he came back it was
with an army five times as large as David's band. David was still using
caves for his men and his supplies. One day, David and a few men were
in the back of a cave when a silhouette appeared at the mouth of the
cave. It was just one man and he had just come in to relieve himself.
They realized after a bit that it was Saul himself. They could see him.
He could not see them. Very embarrassing!

David's men became quite excited. What an opportunity! They
urged David to go ahead and kill him and argued that this was a
God-given chance. God had put Saul in David's power. David crept
forward quietly but only to cut off a piece of Saul's robe. His men
were astounded. What was he thinking about? It was the chance of a
lifetime and David was throwing it away. They were ready to do what
David refused to do.

For David it was his conscience that was troubling him. There was
a principle at stake. Saul had been chosen as King by God and Samuel
had anointed him to the office before the people. David could not

bring himself to harm him in any way. He explained this to his men and with difficulty persuaded them from taking the law into their own hands. All this happened within a few minutes.

OPPORTUNITY DOES NOT NEGATE PRINCIPLES

It is easy to interpret providential happenings so that they support what you want to do anyway. David's men fell into that trap. They even misquoted something they imagined God had said to back up their view. For David, however, opportunity did not cancel principles and he let the opportunity pass.

POPULAR SUPPORT DOES NOT OVERRIDE PRINCIPLES

David had 600 good and loyal men supporting him and they would have agreed with the few men in the cave who urged David to kill Saul. David would not do it. David, however, did not subscribe to the common concept of leadership, 'find out what the people want and lead them to it'. He did not say, as many do in effect, "I am your leader; I will follow you." He did not abdicate from his principle just because he had popular support.

Instead of violence he tried talking. Long before Winston Churchill said he preferred Jaw to war, David engaged Saul in dialogue. He followed Saul out of the cave and confronted him verbally: both men made a speech and important things were said.

I AM NOT A REBEL

'Why do you listen to people who say that I am trying to harm you? You can see for yourself that just now in the cave the LORD put you in my power. Some of my men told me to kill you, but I felt sorry for you and said that I would not harm you in the least, because you are the one whom the LORD chose to be king. Look, my father, look at the piece of your robe I am holding! I could have killed you, but instead I only cut this off. This should convince you that I have no thought of rebelling against you or of harming you.' In the dialogue, his refusal to use violence in the cave added great force to what he was saying about not being a rebel.

In addition, the whole tone of David's speech was respectful. He calls Saul, 'Your majesty!' and bows down to the ground to honour him. He even refers to Saul as, 'My father!' To reinforce this he speaks of himself as of little significance, a dead dog or a flea, not worth chasing. He is content to leave the judgment on Saul's conduct to the LORD (1 Sam. 24:9-15).

YOU WILL BE KING!

It works! Saul is overcome with deep emotion and even weeps. He responds to David's 'My father' with, 'David, my son!' He recognizes that David is in the right and he is in the wrong. He marvels at David's unbelievable restraint in the cave. He even goes so far as to say, 'You will be king of Israel' and only asks that when he is king he be kind to his descendants so that his name will not be forgotten (1 Sam. 24:16-21).

This is the second confirmation that David has had of what Samuel told him right at the beginning of the story. Jonathan had said it and even suggested that his father knew it too. Here Saul confirms what Jonathan had hinted at (1 Sam. 23:17). David was achieving his goal without using violence. For the time being Saul called off the manhunt.

THE SOURCE OF AUTHORITY

David's principle of loyalty to God's appointed leader implied a philosophy of history that saw God as the ultimate authority and controller of events. From the beginning, the God of Israel stands before us as one God – invisible Creator of all things, ruler of nature and of history. The Psalms announce it, 'You are the one who judges. You can take away power and give it to others' (Ps. 75:7), and more generally, 'The LORD is King!'

The prophet Daniel stated it to Nebuchadnezzar: 'God is wise and powerful! Praise him for ever and ever. He controls the times and the seasons; he makes and unmakes kings; it is he who gives wisdom and understanding' (Dan. 2:20-21). Jesus had the same outlook when Pilate said to him, '"Remember, I have the authority to set you free and also to have you crucified." Jesus answered, "You have authority over me only because it was given to you by God"' (John 19:10-11).

The Apostle Paul restated this concept in the New Testament: 'Everyone must obey the state authorities, because no authority exists without God's permission, and the existing authorities have been put there by God' (Rom. 13:1).

David based his principle on a conviction that runs throughout the Bible: God ultimately controls history. Governments are primarily God's concern, and David had no wish to abrogate to himself what he felt belonged to God.

David not only refused to forget his principle and kill Saul, he also worked in every way possible to show his positive attitude to Saul's whole family. David cherished his friendship with Saul's son Jonathan. He regarded as inviolate his marriage to Saul's daughter Michal even after Saul was dead (2 Sam. 3:14-16). When Saul's son Ishbosheth was made king of the northern part of the country by his general, Abner, David took no action against him except to defend himself when attacked. When eventually both the general and Ishbosheth were assassinated, he disassociated himself from both acts in the strongest possible language (2 Sam. 3-4). When he himself ruled over the whole country, he sought out Saul's lame grandson Mephibosheth and brought him to the palace and maintained him all his life. David consistently acted towards Saul's family on the principle of generosity and loyalty.

THE VALIDITY OF HIS PRINCIPLE

Sticking to his convictions did not come easily, but David's adherence to this principle became a binding force in the nation. David saw clearly the need to build unity. He wanted to win and not antagonize the tribe of Benjamin, who had given Israel their first king. What would any tribe think if one of their people was the ruler and a man from another tribe assassinated him and took over the government? Africa in the 1960s provides the answer. The civil war in Nigeria had just such moves underlying it, and the hatred and antagonism engendered will take generations to work out. Sudan, Togo, Dahomey, Gabon, Zanzibar, Ghana, the Congo and Sierra Leone, all have seen the army usurp the civilian government and take over the running of their countries. In other countries abortive military mutinies have been quelled. But David rejected this violent path to power, and it is significant that half a century later, when the country was again divided, Benjamin was the one tribe that stayed with Judah while the other ten seceded (1 Kings 12:21-24). Even after he was dead, his waiting patiently for God's help and his adherence to the principle of loyalty to the God-appointed ruler were remarkably rewarded.

David had not heard Jesus say, 'All who take the sword will die by the sword' (Matt. 26:52). This implies what is by now obvious that when you use violence you start off a chain reaction and you can not know where it is going to end. The French Revolution is probably the greatest example in history. The violence of the early revolutionaries was turned on themselves and eventually France became an empire again.

David did not know that Jesus would refuse to sanction violence even when he was unjustly arrested. He had no inkling of the resurrection that made him, the victim, the victor. Yet he as the victim in this case also became the victor, with a similar confidence in God that kept him true to his principle to the end, and built an element of stability into the nation's life.

TODAY'S CHALLENGES:

The corrupting power of wealth.
Losing your temper.
Listening to women.
Breaking the revenge cycle.

'But now I tell you: do not take revenge
on someone who wrongs you.'
(Matt. 5:39)

10
Kept From Taking Revenge

1 Samuel 25

A MAJOR TEMPTATION

Saul seems to have left David alone for awhile but David stayed on
with his men in the wilderness, far away from national events like the
death of the prophet Samuel (1 Sam. 24:22–25:1). Life took on a less
frenetic pace and his men found things to keep themselves occupied
and supplied with life's necessities. They took it on themselves to
protect local farmers from cattle thieves. In this period of relative
calm David was confronted with a major temptation.

One beneficiary of their protection was a man called Nabal.
He had 4,000 cattle, 3,000 sheep, 1,000 goats, all with access to
the extensive pasture-land needed to graze them (1 Sam. 25:2-3).
He was descended from the old aristocratic family of Caleb. By
any standards he was extremely rich. His lands, however, were
set in an area in which stock theft was a major hazard both from
local people and raiding parties from neighbouring peoples.
Saul's government in Israel was weak, and security in the area was
ineffective. David and his outlawed band of 600 men provided this
in true Robin Hood style. A good relationship developed between

Nabal's herdsmen and David's soldiers. Feeding 600 men on the run was no easy task and, not unnaturally, David received gifts in kind from the farms that owed their security and prosperity to him.

One year, when it was sheepshearing time for Nabal's 3,000 sheep, and in anticipation of the customary feast, David sent out ten of his young men to the farm with this message, 'David sends you greetings, my friend, with his best wishes for you, your family, and all that is yours. He heard that you were shearing your sheep, and he wants you to know that your shepherds have been with us and we did not harm them. Nothing that belonged to them was stolen... Just ask them, and they will tell you. We have come on a feast day, and David asks you to receive us kindly. Please give what you can to us your servants and to your dear friend David' (1 Sam. 25:6-8). It was not much to ask, especially in a society where traditionally the poor were provided for at harvest time (Lev. 23:22).

THE RICH FOOL OF THE OLD TESTAMENT

Nabal, however, was a prototype of the man in the New Testament who says to himself, 'Lucky man! You have all the good things you need for many years. Take life easy, eat, drink, and enjoy yourself!' but who is never satisfied (Luke 12:19). When Nabal heard their little speech, he came out in his true colours. At the best of times, he was churlish and evil (AV), surly and mean (NIV), brutish and ill-mannered (JB), mean and bad tempered (GNB) (1 Sam. 25:3).

He speaks for himself. 'David, who is he?' He was impressed, if not obsessed, with his own origins. He was a descendant of the great Caleb (Num. 13; Josh. 14). He was of the aristocracy in Judah. He knew where he came from. He was true blue Judah. This David had Moabite blood in him if the rumours were correct. His great-grandmother Ruth had been from Moab.

Nabal's was a great inheritance. Sometimes a great inheritance can be oppressive because it always has to be lived up to. What is a great start can progressively cripple the personality with a sense of falling short. This makes the person judgmental and critical of others to keep pushing their own inadequacy out of mind.

It leads them also to put the worst construction on the successes of other people. No doubt Nabal had heard his wife and all her young female friends singing the praises of David after he defeated the giant Goliath. Young upstart! When he fell from favour at the court of King Saul, no doubt Nabal said 'I told you so.' Now David was in Nabal's own district as an outlaw. This enabled him in his mind to brand David as just another runaway slave. That is how it came out when David's men tried to talk as though David were a friend whom he could assist with some provisions. The suggestion that he was indebted to David for the security of his herds was anathema to him. He was capable of seeing to his own security.

People like Nabal are excessively proud and possessive of what they have done. It offsets their deeper and hidden feelings of inadequacy. 'I'm not going to take my bread and water, and the animals I have slaughtered for my shearers, and give them to men who come from I don't know where!' He fell right into the trap that Moses warned them to avoid. Don't think that it has been your hand that has got you where you are. It is to God's grace and goodness that we owe everything and we should remember that. The servants tell us how he reacted. He 'flew upon' David's men, 'flared out at them' (JB), 'snarled and snapped at them' (Josephus), 'hurled insults at them' (NIV) (1 Sam. 25:14).

His wife later summed him up with two words, 'good-for-nothing' and 'fool' (1 Sam. 25:25), which is a terrible indictment from a spouse. The same term is used by the servants who expand on it by saying, 'no one can talk to him'. He just did not listen. It is no wonder that his wife did not always tell him what she was doing (1 Sam. 25:19, 36-39). It is often all you can do if a person does not listen. David felt insulted, reproached and treated with contempt.

A DEVIL AT HOME

It was not pleasant. It showed what an ill-natured, ill-tempered, ill-mannered, boorish and badly behaved man he was. He stepped straight into the character of the big-mouthed, swaggering miser, eloquent in expletives, of which almost any literature has its example. Success and prosperity had been his great test. It could have made him a better man, but it made him worse. He was successful in farming. He had a good-looking wife, but he still did not have enough. He should have been expanding with the easier circumstances, becoming more relaxed, more friendly, more generous and more approachable. Instead he became harder, more cocksure and arrogant, more self-centred and grasping, more stubborn and loud-mouthed, and more of a fool, which is what Nabal means.

His sheepshearing feast was princely, but only for his own benefit. It would seem that his wife did not matter very much to him. Once he had her, he took her for granted; she could be away from the house and the feast, and he did not even notice. At the end of the story when his wife told him how she had saved them all from disaster, he did not thank her but had a fit, went into a coma and died ten days later from the shock.

Nabal's character is clear. From our knowledge of his many counterparts, we can imagine him regularly fulminating over Abigail's extravagance and waste in her house-keeping, and at the same time wanting fine fare served daily. No doubt he was adept at casting aspersions on Abigail's family and regarding them in his self-righteousness as immoral scum. When she kept quiet (perhaps the only way she knew how to cope) he would rage because he was not answered.

His servants would suffer from his unjust accusations about theft, their lack of character, their origins and their work. The only thing worse than his tirades would be his sullen silences when everyone feared what would burst from the cloud that was forming about his brow. Nabal was his name, and folly was with him.

Nabal is an extreme case. I hope we can say that we are not all like that. I hope, however, that we will all say that we are a bit like that sometimes. Maybe we need to notice if we are on the way to becoming like that and take action.

'A devil at home' is one of Thomas Shepherd's descriptions of the evangelical hypocrite. He is referring to the kind of person who is a prominent Christian outside but sits silent at meals and behaving in such a way as to make everyone else feel rotten.

A PATIENT MAN LOSES CONTROL

When David's men returned with Nabal's answer, David was furious. He would be about twenty-eight years of age. His mentor, the prophet Samuel, has just died. It is unlikely that he would go to the great funeral. He was an outlaw. Samuel was a great loss and David must have felt very vulnerable and exposed.

The Nabal incident is recorded just after the occasion (chapter 24) when David showed uncommon restraint and refused to take revenge on Saul when he was very much in his power. Although he had been able to keep his head under the great stress of being unjustly pursued by Saul, this small man, Nabal, took him off his guard. Although he had been careful to restrain his men from taking any action that would injure the King, he was stung into mobilizing them for the merciless massacre of all on Nabal's farm very soon afterward. Although Nabal had not done anything to him yet, except be nasty to his servants, he was ready to take extreme measures to deal with him.

He was about to answer the fool according to his folly. He committed himself to revenge, even if it meant the murder of innocent people. We can see it all in the turmoil of his inner thoughts: 'Why did I ever protect that fellow's property out here in the wilderness? Not a thing that belonged to him was stolen, and this is how he pays me back for the help I gave him! May God strike me dead if I don't kill every last one of those men before morning!' (1 Sam. 25:21-22). Mercifully, there was someone thinking straight that day.

Our anger needs to be managed. We live in an angry age. We have all kinds of new rages springing up like road rage, domestic rage, etc. Anger is the precursor of violence and we will not succeed in combating violence until we have a way to reduce anger.

A WIFE FIT FOR A KING

All was not folly in Nabal's household. Abigail, his wife saved the day. Her name means the joy of her father. Nabal and Abigail are about the strangest combination of husband and wife one could ever imagine. How they could ever have come to be mated defies speculation. On the surface it seems as though that was the one occasion on which her intelligence failed her. Why did she marry him? Did she marry the money? Was it an arranged marriage? Was he a good actor, playing the noble suitor until he got what he wanted? Perhaps he was different as a suitor. Whatever the reason, she had made her bed and had to lie on it. The amazing thing is that she did not become sour with him.

This incident shows what stuff she was made of. She was a person of decisive action. She knew her stock and her kitchen and had supplies laid in to cope with emergencies. She had her servants' complete confidence. They would do anything for her. It was one of them who reported to her what had transpired between David and Nabal.

She did not lose a minute. She organized her party and her goods with arithmetical precision for David's men: 5 sheep, 5 sacks of grain, 100 bushels of raisins, 200 loaves of bread, 200 cakes of dried figs and 2 large leather bags of wine. She was so well organized, the heart of her husband might well have trusted in her! She loaded it all on donkeys, sent it ahead with her servants to pacify David's anger, and came later with all her wisdom and charm.

It was a classic meeting. She made the longest recorded speech of any woman in the Bible. She somehow anticipated that David was destined to be king. All that she said was motivated by what she knew was necessary for a future king.

Her 300 words (English) are a veritable gem of a public relations exercise. Practitioners today give rules for influencing people without giving offence, but without having read those books she used all the rules!

*Talk about your own mistakes before criticising the other person:
'Please, sir, listen to me! Let me take the blame. Please, don't pay any attention to Nabal, that good-for-nothing! He is exactly what his name means a fool! I wasn't there when your servants arrived, sir' (1 Sam. 25:24-25).

* Call attention to the other's mistakes indirectly:
'It is the LORD who has kept you from taking revenge and killing your enemies. And now I swear to you by the living LORD that your enemies and all who want to harm you will be punished like Nabal' (1 Sam. 25:26).

* Make the fault seem easy to correct:
'Please, sir, accept this present I have brought you, and give it to your men' (1 Sam. 25:27).

* Use honest appreciation:
'Please, forgive me, sir, for any wrong I have done. The Lord will make you king, and your descendants also, because you are fighting his battles' (1 Sam. 25:28). Abigail was the fourth person who affirmed that David would become king.

* Give the dog a good name, a reputation to live up to:
'[Y]ou will not do anything evil as long as you live. If anyone should attack you and try to kill you, the LORD your God will keep you safe, as a man guards a precious treasure. As for your enemies, however, he will throw them away, as a man hurls stones with his catapult' (1 Sam. 25:28-29).

* Let the other man save his face:
'And when the LORD has done all the good things he has promised you and has made you king of Israel, then you will not have to feel regret or remorse, sir, for having killed without cause or for having taken your own revenge. And when the LORD has blessed you, sir, please do not forget me' (1 Sam. 25:30-31).

* Make the other person happy at the thing you suggest:
'David said to her, "Praise the LORD, the God of Israel, who sent you today to meet me! Thank God for your good sense and for what you have done today in keeping me from the crime of murder and from taking my own revenge" (1 Sam. 25:32-33).

With all her womanly skill, she did not hesitate to admit her husband's faults. Yet, she defended him both by what she did and how she did it. Although, she felt it wise not to advise him of her intentions beforehand (1 Sam. 25:19).

HER THEOLOGY:

Apart from David's oath about what he was going to do to Nabal (v.22) there is no mention of God in this story until Abigail steps into the frame. Then the LORD is in almost every verse. She clearly lived before the LORD in her own mind and heart.

What God did she believe in? She called him the LORD, i.e. Yahweh or Jehovah, the only God, the one who causes to be what comes into existence. This was the God of Israel who had revealed himself to Moses at the burning bush. He was the Living LORD (v.26) not a lifeless image, a LORD who restrains people like David from doing wrong. He makes kings (v.28). keeps promises, (v.30). blesses his people, (v.31).

HER MORALITY:

Her morality sprang from her theology. She believed in prompt, practical and generous gratitude. She prepared the supplies for David's men out of the food set aside for the feast. She was confident enough in God to act on her own against her husband when the occasion called for it. She saw taking revenge as wrong and especially if it involves killing people without cause (vv.26, 31). Evil was to be shunned (v.26). She was concerned about consequences, political and other (v.31). '[Y]ou will not have to feel regret'. She had good sense, as David admitted (v.32).

VENGEANCE ABANDONED

David's words in response are almost a mirror image of what Abigail has said to him. He uses all the same words that she had used. He obviously believed in the same God that she believed in, even if he had forgotten him for the moment. It was a major climb down. It was not difficult for him to climb down as we can see in his behaviour before Saul in the previous chapter. He had just had an almost fatal moral lapse in a time when his defences were down. We often think of Old Testament (OT) times as times that believed in an angry God.

That is something of a caricature. Right from Sinai, God describes himself as 'slow to anger, abounding in love and faithfulness'. In the law, vengeance, where it was due, had to be limited only to an eye for an eye and a tooth for a tooth. The cities of refuge were designated to make sure that vengeance did not violate justice. Even in the New Testament (NT) when Paul is arguing against taking vengeance it is to OT passages that he appeals. 'Never take revenge, my friends, but instead let God's anger do it. For the scripture says, "I will take revenge, I will pay back, says the Lord"' (Rom. 12:19; see Lev. 19:18; Deut. 32:35).

This is the issue that is raised by this story. David had been deterred from harming Saul because he would not lift his hand against the LORD's anointed. Now Abigail was showing him that the principle is of more universal application. It even applies where people are least deserving of consideration. The reason for the ban is the after-effects on the person taking the vengeance and the continuance of the cycle of hatred and bitterness.

Jesus takes it further, 'You have heard that it was said, "An eye for an eye, and a tooth for a tooth." But now I tell you: do not take revenge on someone who wrongs you.'

THE OUTCOME

Abigail did tell Nabal what she had done at the earliest suitable moment in the morning after the feast and hid nothing (1 Sam. 25:36-37). It was too much for mean, miserly Nabal. Instead of thanking her for her timely intervention, he had a stroke and died. Scripture does not specifically reveal what gave him his stroke, but it shows how foolishly his heart was imprisoned by his miserliness.

Neither Abigail's resourcefulness, intelligence, beauty or faith were lost on David. A person who could so quickly penetrate through his foolish temper and point out where his real interests lie was a person worth having around. When he heard that Nabal had died, he proposed marriage, and she accepted. How much she influenced the man he became is not known. David's was not a happy household, and undoubtedly she had plenty of opportunity to show her resourcefulness and many more tempers to cool. We do know, however, that neither she nor her children figure in the later, more sordid doings of David's unhappy court.

TODAY'S CHALLENGES:

Not letting others take the blame.
Sticking to principles.
The secrets of patience.

'Jesus said to them, "The right time for me has not yet come."
(John 7:6)

11

A Lifetime of Waiting

1 Samuel 26

WAITING FOR A DEAD MAN'S SHOES

There is a certain monotony, a sense of déjà vu, about the David story in 1 Samuel 26. Sometime ago he had been given a reprieve and was no longer hunted by Saul. He was not, however, invited back to the court or given a position in the army. We are not surprised that David still did not trust Saul. David kept his band together and they became an unofficial protection force for the farmers in the countryside. Samuel the prophet had died and his passing was a loss to everyone. For David, Samuel was the only one who could authenticate his call to be king. In this period also he married Abigail, his first real wife. Life was all very settled, not to say boring.

Then the pace quickened again. It may have been that the death of Samuel unsettled Saul and made him feel that David and his militia could not be allowed to be there indefinitely. Something made the men of Ziph get up to their old tricks and they sent men to the palace with news of David's whereabouts. Saul responded in the old style and sent 3,000 troops to capture or kill him.

David got wind of this and, like any good commander, sent out spies who confirmed that Saul was indeed on the move. David lost no time in going to where the army was camped. He asked for a volunteer to go with him in a night sortie into the camp. His stepsister's son Abishai went with him.

They had no difficulty making their way right to where Saul was sleeping. Everyone was in an unnaturally deep sleep. Abishai wanted to take Saul's spear and kill him there and then. To him it was another God-given opportunity, but it provoked a very revealing whispered conversation between the two men. David had clearly got his spirit of revenge and tendency to violence under control again after the Nabal incident. He reiterated to Abishai his commitment not to harm the man God had chosen to be king. In doing so, however, he revealed his mindset. 'I know that the LORD himself will kill Saul, either when his time comes to die a natural death or when he dies in battle.' David was resigned to wait until Saul died before advancing any claim to the throne. It was taking a very long time but he did not waver in his conviction.

A TEMPTING OFFER

As they stood over the sleeping Saul and Abner, Abishai said, 'Now let me plunge his own spear through him and pin him to the ground with just one blow I won't have to strike twice!' (1 Sam. 26:8). Abishai's offer to spear Saul put David into another temptation. David was unwilling to kill Saul himself, but if Abishai was willing to do the dirty work and to take the blame, was that different? Abishai no doubt understood the political risks for David. He was willing to risk banishment or imprisonment for his master, confident that when David came to power he would make things right. David need never soil his hands in this affair. David, however, refused his offer; he did not imagine that by turning away his head while the deed was done that he would not be implicated. Unlike Pilate at the crucifixion of

Jesus, David would not take a basin, wash his hands, and say, 'All right, you do it. I am innocent.'

CONTROLLING HIS REACTION

Saul had ignored his promise to leave David alone. He returned with his army to the Desert of Ziph to hunt him down again. David refused to harm him in spite of the fact that he had broken his word. Many other men would have regarded himself as free from any obligation to keep faith. David's principle, however, was held before God, and man's unreliability only reinforced his need to be true. Not even Saul's treachery made him feel justified in retaliating in kind.

THAT SPEAR!

'Let's take his spear and go,' he said. This could have been the spear that Saul had hurled at David to kill him earlier in his life. It was quite a symbol for him to take it now. The two men went to the top of a hill close by and shouted to waken the whole army. David and Abner, Saul's commander, bandied words about Saul's missing spear when Saul woke up and recognized David's voice. 'Is that you, my son?'

David's answer again reveals his thinking. He cannot understand why Saul is after him again. Have other people put Saul up to it? If they have, 'They have driven me out from the LORD's land to a country where I can only worship foreign gods. Don't let me be killed on foreign soil, away from the LORD.' He is feeling he cannot carry on as he has been doing. It is taking too long to wait for Saul to die. He might have to consider exile and he dreads that. Nonetheless, he sticks to his principle of loyalty to God's anointed king. He just tells someone to come and collect the fateful spear.

WAITING ON THE LORD

The dream that Samuel inspired in David was taking forever to materialise. That was not easy for him. He was getting desperate.

After some months of quiet when he was able to be of some use to some people, the perpetual running away and dodging capture was back. It was agony. Yet, he still had to wait. In fact he was not just waiting for Saul to die although it may have seemed like it. Inwardly he was learning about waiting on God. We learn this from the language he uses in the Psalms. In about a dozen of his poems he talks about waiting on the Lord, when he does it, what it does for him and how good it feels when the waiting comes to an end.

He says in Psalm 40, 'I waited patiently for the LORD's help; then he listened to me and heard my cry. He pulled me out of a dangerous pit, out of the deadly quicksand. He set me safely on a rock and made me secure. 'He taught me to sing a new song, a song of praise to our God.'

He learned about waiting on God from looking around at the way God works in nature. God does not just start to work when we ask him. He is providing for everybody all the time (Ps. 104:27-28; 145:14-15). So, he may be trusted to provide for us too.

Waiting on God leads to discovering his ways, maintaining our integrity and avoiding shame (Ps. 25:3-5, 21). It is the best way to keep up your courage (Ps. 27:14; 31:24). Sometimes you do not know what you are waiting for and at other times you wait in desperation (Ps. 39:7, 8; 130:5, 6).

Part of it is a matter of timing. You wait on God for the right time. Isaiah says that if we wait on the LORD, we will mount up with wings as eagles. The picture is of the eagle hovering until it finds itself in an upward current of hot air and then it soars aloft with little effort.

At this stage, however, his impatience was building up to unbearable proportions. He longed for things to change, to improve. And it was not happening. He became tired of waiting, as we shall see, and we have no record of him praying.

TODAY'S CHALLENGES:

Betraying one's country.
Getting rich quick.
The mercenary motive.

Jesus said, 'whoever wants to save
his own life will lose it...'
What shall it profit a man if he gain
the whole world and lose his own soul?'
(Luke 9:24-25)

12

The Mercenary

1 Samuel 27 & 29

A COUNSEL OF DESPAIR

There are some really low points in the career of David. One of them
came towards the end of his outlaw period. The long pursuit was
wearing him down. Looking after a growing band of men who were
already discontented or in some kind of distress was taking its toll. In
spite of three serious attempts to effect some kind of reconciliation
with Saul, the situation did not improve. It was getting David
down. He had no desire to lead an opposition group, or a resistance
movement, or a subversive gang. But the way Saul handled things left
him in a dilemma. What should he do?

Palestine was very unstable. Egypt was the world power that had
such hegemony as there was over the area. The five Philistine cities
had the most military muscle in the southern end of the country but
it was nothing like a settled occupation. The books of Samuel mention
about nine other ethnic or city-based groups that were part of the
struggles of the region. A feature of the period was the availability of
small mercenary armies who were ready, for a price, to fight for one
or other of the groups who lived there.

Should David disband his small army of friends and malcontents who had rallied to him and try to survive on his own, somewhere, as an individual? He said to himself, 'One of these days Saul will kill me. The best thing for me to do is to escape to Philistia. Then Saul will give up looking for me in Israel, and I will be safe' (1 Sam. 27:1). He did it, but with all his men.

Now the Philistines were public enemy number one as far as Israel was concerned. So David was making a decision to go over to the other side when he virtually hired himself and his private army of 600 men to Achish, king of the city state of Gath in the Gaza strip. He was becoming a mercenary with his own loyal army. He was becoming a turncoat and being disloyal to his own people.

What are mercenaries? They are men who hire themselves out to fight for pay for a government or leader other than their own. The Regulation of Foreign Military Assistance Act 1998 in South Africa defines mercenary activity as 'Direct participation as a combatant in armed conflict for private gain'. Mercenaries are as old as war itself. They have been less used since the rise of the nation state with their own standing armies able and ready to fight for the nation to which they belong. They have come back into prominence again in recent times. They figured prominently in the 1960s in Africa where newly independent states dissolved into civil wars, notably in Congo. In the new millennium, in west Africa, young veterans of the wars there are being recruited to fight new conflicts in the region, according to reports by the Human Rights Watch. Poverty is forcing thousands of young men and boys to become mercenaries. Fighters are moving freely between conflicts in Liberia, Sierra Leone, Guinea and the Ivory Coast. A veteran of several wars in west Africa said he fought to support his parents. 'The commander said we could pay ourselves, which meant looting,' he told Human Rights Watch.

This is the category into which David moved when he went over to Achish, King of Gath. No doubt he felt driven to it by the frustrations he was experiencing. There was no opportunity to use his considerable ability in the service of his own country. This is usually how mercenaries are made. There is some lack in the society they come from, some vacuum in their personal lives. Some bitterness in their previous experience provides the thrust that makes many of them sell themselves to fight for the party that will give the highest pay.

Bitterness was creeping up on David. We have the impression that God was receding into the background. There is no mention of God or any record of David consulting the LORD either through a priest or in any other way. He felt alone and so reverted to his own strategies. He had already expressed his worry about being driven into an idolatrous society (1 Sam. 26:19).

A COURSE OF DUPLICITY

Once David had made the decision to become a mercenary, a number of other things also began to deteriorate. Truth became the first casualty. To begin with, David's private army was stationed in the royal city of Gath under the watchful eye of the King. David's men, accustomed to the free life of adventurers, soon chafed under this restriction. To deal with this situation, David made a convincing argument to the King about his people causing too much inconvenience in Gath. He suggested that they be moved to another, smaller town. Achish was taken in and said that they could be stationed at Ziklag, some miles further south.

Once they had escaped the supervision of Achish, David quickly set to work. He sent men out to raid tribes further south who were traditional enemies of Israel. In these raids his men acquired considerable booty of sheep, oxen, asses, camels and clothing. Raiding neighbours was part of the economy of that part of the world. This is the closest that David ever came to getting rich. Whenever Achish called and saw the increasing livestock, he asked where David had raided this time. Invariably David kept a straight face and lied that he had raided one of the settlements in the south of Judah or one of her allies. David and his men prospered, but truth became a casualty.

Respect for life also suffered. In order to conceal his lies to Achish, people were indiscriminately massacred. David strictly instructed his men to put everyone, men, women and children to the sword. No one was to be left alive to tell the tale.

During this period David clearly lowered the value that he set on personal relationships. He professed allegiance to Achish, and Achish trusted him. Totally deceived about the source of David's increasing wealth, the Philistine king made him his permanent bodyguard. When his fellow Philistine commanders challenged his trust of David, Achish defended him: 'He has been with me for quite a long time now. He has done nothing I can find fault with since the day he came over to me'. To David himself Achish said, 'I consider you as loyal as an angel of God' (1 Sam. 29:3, 9).

Nothing else in David's career matched the murderous, cheating, hoodwinking skulduggery of the sixteen months that he spent at Ziklag. No doubt David rationalized his behaviour. He was fighting Israel's enemies. He was protecting his men from Saul, increasing their wealth, consolidating his position after years on the run. He had never had it so good before. After he had once begun to be controlled by the mercenary spirit, any number of good reasons must have seemed to support his actions.

All through this period, the only mention of God comes from the lips of the heathen king Achish when he naïvely protests David's honesty (1 Sam. 29:6, 9). At this time David wrote no psalms. He seems to have hung up his harp and lost his song. When David forgot God, the spirit of seeking personal advantage began to undermine the things that made him great.

A CLIMAX OF DISILLUSIONMENT

Although the provocation was strong to adopt the creed of the mercenary, the consequences were nearly disastrous. The time came when the Philistines prepared to march on Israel, and Achish said to David, 'Of course you understand that you and your men are to fight on my side' (1 Sam. 28:1). David had deserted to keep from fighting Saul; now he was being forced by the way that he had lived by for sixteen months to go into the Philistine front line against Saul and all Israel. He found himself on the wrong side.

Mercifully, the other Philistine commanders did not want to risk having traitors in their ranks and asked, 'What are these Hebrews doing here?' and insisted that they be sent back (1 Sam. 29:3). David's former prowess under Saul was well known, and his new allegiance was suspect.

He was now disowned by both sides, in a spiritual desert with nowhere to go but back. He had played out his deceptions, and they recoiled on his own head and shamed his benefactor. He was at an all-time low and might well have disappeared as another one who showed great promise but went the way of all flesh, drowning his potential glory in the flood of self-interest.

At this point there was little to choose between David and Saul. Neither seemed to provide hope for Israel. Both were on the track of self-interest. It was a dangerous and a downward track, but the end was not yet. The consequences of self-interest were nearly disastrous.

THE MERCENARY SPIRIT

I believe this is the story of all mercenaries but I do not believe that all mercenaries are soldiers. Our language does not either. For we say a person has a mercenary spirit who may never have been near a gun. They are people who will do anything for personal advantage in their lives. They desert their parents like the prodigal Son. They turn their backs on their leader and their friends and desert their cause like Judas. Like Demas, they become enamoured of what this world has to offer and forsake Christ and the gospel. They profess to be giving to God what is going in to their own bank account like Ananias and Sapphira.

Politicians, civil servants, business men and Trade union leaders can all move over from good beginnings to making their own survival or advantage their primary concern. Wives and husbands, Christian ministers and evangelists, can abandon loyalty and be wholly controlled by the bottom line. Even nurses, students and scholars, and professional people like doctors, dentists, lawyers and teachers can adopt the mercenary spirit.

We have all seen people who begin with great ideals and idealism but change over time to something very different. We agree with Lord Acton who said, 'Power tends to corrupt and absolute power corrupts absolutely.' I was asked recently what it was that gets corrupted. I answered that it is our attitude that gets undermined. The attitude of survival at all costs, or prosperity at all costs, displaces the attitude of rectitude and concern for others' welfare.

David was heading for near absolute power. It was probably a mercy that he confronted this side of his nature before he reached that place. Mercifully he did not stay down and we are about to learn how he rose again.

TODAY'S CHALLENGES:

What would we do if we lost everything?
What would we do if we got it all back?
Holding property and possessions lightly.

Jesus said, 'My Father, if it is possible,
take this cup of suffering from me!
Yet not what I want, but what you want.'
(Matt. 26:39)

13

Out of the Depths

1 Samuel 30

HIS OWN MEDICINE

David had one step lower to go. He had been outlawed and hounded out of Israel by Saul. He was rejected by the Philistines and excluded from the ranks of their fighting men. All he had left were his own men and they turned on him also. This is how it happened.

Sent away by the suspicious Philistine leaders, he made his way back to Ziklag, which had been their base in recent times. The town was a smoking ruin. The wives and children of all his men had been taken captive, his two wives among them. All their livestock and goods had been plundered; there was nothing and nobody left.

There had been a raid by some Amalekites, one of the peoples that he and his men had plundered in their own raids from Ziklag (1 Sam. 27:8). No doubt it was a reprisal for the raids they had suffered, and apparently David had left their families without adequate protection so the Amalekites were able to carry off all their goods and the women and children as slaves.

All seemed lost: 'David and his men started crying and did not stop until they were completely exhausted.' It is hardly imaginable to think of 600 husbands and fathers discovering at the same time that all their wives and children had disappeared, and might be dead. They collapsed into an agonizing corporate lament. It turned into a Mournfest. Only when they had exhausted their grief did they begin to think. What they thought was not good for David. It was a sense of loss, betrayal, anger, fury. 'David was now in great trouble, because his men were all very bitter about losing their children, and they were threatening to stone him' (1 Sam. 30:4, 6).

A more lonely person is hard to imagine. If he had sowed the wind, he was now reaping the whirlwind. The raider had been raided. All he had accumulated was gone. Not a shred remained and his men turned on him threatening a slow, cruel death by stoning. For the first time he was completely helpless. He had failed in everything he set out to do, and he had a mocking conscience that told him that he was only being given his own medicine. He had asked for it all. He alone was responsible. Failure is a great test of any person. What did David do?

BACK TO THE LORD

David strengthened himself in the LORD, his God (1 Sam. 30:6). He turned right around to what he had long known but recently ignored. He opened heart, mind, soul and strength to God. There was no one else to whom he could go but to the LORD, and he was humble enough to go. We do not have the exact prayer he used, but its elements must have been something like what he wrote in Psalm 143.

> LORD, hear my prayer! In your righteousness listen to my plea;
> answer me in your faithfulness!
> Don't put me, your servant, on trial;
> no one is innocent in your sight.
> My enemy has hunted me down and completely defeated me.
> He has put me in a dark prison,
> and I am like those who died long ago.
> So I am ready to give up; I am in deep despair…

> My prayers go up to you; show me the way I should go.
> I go to you for protection, LORD; rescue me from my enemies.
> You are my God; teach me to do your will.
> Be good to me, and guide me on a safe path.
> Rescue me, LORD, as you have promised;
> in your goodness save me from my troubles!

Whatever the words David used, the change was immediate. He called the priest who had served him in earlier days and urged him to ask the LORD whether or not he should go after the raiders. This was an amazing change! He was ready to pursue and recover what had been taken or, if the LORD wished, to stay and accept his loss and along with it, perhaps, even the threat of death by stoning.

If the mark of true repentance is the willingness to face and accept the consequences of our actions, David was repentant that day at Ziklag. He was ready to bear with meekness the hand of God. He did not struggle to assert himself or move heaven and earth to get back to where he had been.

He and his men waited for Abiathar the priest to indicate the mind of the LORD. It was a tense moment on which hung issues of life or death, and the fulfilment or the denial of the promise of God to David that he would be king. The word came back, 'Go after them; you will catch them and rescue the captives' (v. 8).

A RELUCTANT GUIDE

With everything and everyone he had, David set off in pursuit. The men, already wearied by the long journey from the Philistine battle lines, were driven to superhuman efforts. As far as David was concerned, he was out to undo, as far as he could, the damage his own conduct had caused. For one-third of the men the demands were too much, and they gave up the chase and stayed behind at a brook called Besor.

Just after that they found an Egyptian starving to death out in the desert. They gave him food and water and discovered that he was a slave who had been part of the raiding party. Reluctantly he agreed to lead them to where the raiders were and they pursued until they caught up with them.

A FATAL PARTY

The raiders were scattered all over the place, eating, drinking and celebrating because of the enormous amount of loot they had captured from Philistia and Judah. At dawn the next day David attacked them and fought until evening. Except for 400 young men who mounted camels and got away, none of them escaped. David rescued everyone and everything the Amalekites had taken, including his two wives; nothing at all was missing. David got back all his men's wives, sons and daughters, and all the loot the Amalekites had taken. He also recovered all the flocks and herds; his men drove all the livestock in front of them and said, 'This belongs to David!'

This was mercy from God, not prowess. David knew this and was learning the lesson. The mercenary mindset raised its head in some of his men on the way back. They wanted to penalise those who had given up the chase out of exhaustion. They could have their wives and children back but they should not get any of the booty. David quickly squashed that idea.

"'My brothers, you can't do this with what the LORD has given us. He kept us safe and gave us victory over the raiders. No one can agree with what you say! All must share alike: whoever stays behind with the supplies gets the same share as the one who goes into battle." David made this a rule, and it has been followed in Israel ever since' (1 Sam. 30:23-25).

The old consideration for others was returning and generosity was not far behind. He sent part of the spoil recovered to the leaders of

Judah in more than a dozen places where he and his men had roamed. The accumulator was becoming the dispenser again.

TWO DEFEATS

It is significant that two defeats took place at the same time. One was this tragedy David suffered at Ziklag. The other was the defeat of Saul and the armies of Israel on Mount Gilboa. Saul's defeat was the end of a long tragic trail of failures. They began with an exaggerated sense of his own importance. This led to an insane and irrational jealousy of David that consumed him for years. Saul did not find repentance. He did not know how to recover from failure and for years had only the semblance of power. He died inwardly years before he was killed in battle and buried.

For David, on the other hand, his defeat was also a kind of death. It was a living death, a dark night of the soul out of which came the resurrection of a different David. This happened before he became king, and the influence of this experience on his coming to the throne was very great. He might have been crowned a proud man and the story might have ended like Saul's. Instead he was crowned a humble man and lived to become a legend to his people for centuries. Ziklag and what happened there was a major key to his greatness.

TODAY'S CHALLENGES:

Refusing to gloat.
Speaking well of the dead.

Jesus said, 'Do for others what
you want them to do for you.'
(Matt. 7:12)

14

Momentous Days

2 Samuel 1

A CROWN ON A PLATE

It all happened at once. David arrived back at Ziklag with the recovered wives, children, goods and livestock. They had hardly settled in and begun to clear up the devastation of their burned homes, when another Amalekite arrived post-haste from the north. He had traveled more than eighty miles to bring the news that the Philistines had defeated the Israelite army at Gilboa. Saul, the king, and Jonathan, his son, were dead.

David asked for the details. The Amalekite said that, when it seemed inevitable that Saul was about to die at the hands of the Philistines, he had asked the Amalekite to kill him. He had done what Saul asked. He took his crown and a bracelet and traveled the eighty miles south to present them to David. No doubt he expected a reward for his pains. A few days earlier, David and his men had temporarily lost their wives, children and goods at Ziklag. They had wept until they had no more strength to weep. But they had recovered everything. Now Saul and Jonathan and the army had been slaughtered by the Philistines at Gilboa and none of them would be coming back.

David was desolate. David was not pleased. David was shocked and mourned Saul and Jonathan's death and fasted until evening.

He accused the Amalekite of killing the LORD's chosen king and had him executed on the spot.

David might have been relieved by Saul's death. He might have said, 'Good riddance!' after all the grief Saul had unjustly caused him. He might have taken the crown and the bracelet, put it on, and declared himself king. He did not.

A TIME TO MOURN

Instead he was inconsolable. It was not a time for words. It was time for song in the most minor of keys. It was not a time for celebration. It was a time for lamentation. He took down his harp and composed a lament. There had been song at his first encounter with Saul when he had soothed the spirit of a very troubled king with his music. Then he charted his scary experiences and his inward struggles by writing psalms in the wilderness. Now at the news of Saul's death, he himself needed a song to soothe his own spirit and the spirit of all Saul's bereaved subjects.

DO NOT SPEAK ILL OF THE DEAD

It is an astonishing poem. He paints the picture of Saul in his early days when he was in the ascendant and routing the Philistines. 'The sword of Saul was merciless, striking down the mighty, killing the enemy. He had been swifter than an eagle, stronger than a lion.' There is not one negative word about Saul. It is an unrelieved lament of David's and the nation's loss. Saul was not just a dead soldier. He was a king who 'clothed the women of Israel in rich scarlet dresses and adorned them with jewels and gold', that gave them dignity. Now he called on them to mourn. Many of them had just been widowed or lost sons or fathers.

By contrast, his imagination told him that the women of Philistia would be singing and dancing with joy as Saul's severed head and his armour were paraded in their cities (1 Sam. 31:9). He knew from his own experience how it went. They had sung about him, 'Saul has killed thousands, but David has killed tens of thousands.' It pained him to think that now the Philistine women were singing and dancing over the death and humiliation of Saul. He wished it were not so, but it was too late to prevent it.

His tribute to Jonathan must have been difficult to compose. 'Saul and Jonathan, so wonderful and dear; together in life, together in death.' David had almost come between father and son but Jonathan did not allow that to happen. He stayed with his father. He argued with him but remained loyal. He fought with him and in the end they died together, not divided. This David celebrates, although it cost him dear to be separated for years from his closest friend. 'I grieve for you, my brother Jonathan; how dear you were to me! How wonderful was your love for me, better even than the love of women.'

REDEEMING THE MEMORY

It is a remarkable lament, but even more remarkable that he ordered it to be taught to the people of his own tribe, Judah, and recorded in the book of Jasher, a collection of national poems referred to in other places in the Bible (2 Sam. 1:17).

Saul was not from Judah. He was from the tribe of Benjamin. David had no influence in Benjamin or the other tribes of Israel. He did, however, have recognition among his own people of Judah. Within a short time they made him their king. One of his first public acts must have been to order that this lament should be taught and sung in Bethlehem, Hebron, and all the towns and hills of Judah.

This was important. He wanted his people to remember the good things about Saul and Jonathan even through the tragic memory of his death and the death of thousands of his brave soldiers on Mount Gilboa. David was providing them with words to express their grief.

He was giving them both permission and a form to process their traumatic experience and come through it ready to face their future. He was bridging the need for positive closure on the past and the need to be open for what the future might bring.

It is noteworthy that there is no mention of God in the lament. There are several laments in the psalms he wrote and they all invoke the LORD, as they were intended for use in the worship of God. Here, however, in composing the song for a controversial figure about whom there would be very different views, he sticks to positive facts and leaves the people to use it within their own frame of reference.

PUBLIC MORALITY

This was one of the greatest acts of public morality in David's career. It could have been so different but he rose to heights of magnanimity that have seldom been equalled. The historian had told the story of Saul, warts and all. In the text, however, David spoke to Saul honestly in life and about him appreciatively in death. In this way he made the path easier that he and others had now to tread.

In 1997, Diana Princess of Wales was killed in a tragic car accident in Paris. A week later there was an unprecedented memorial Service for her in Westminster Abbey. Both there and outside and on the route to her place of burial a whole nation mourned and felt bereft. It was a moving service and it helped many people.

Diana's brother gave a moving eulogy in which he celebrated his sister's life. He put into words what many were thinking and they performed the function of a lament. Sadly, he did not just pay his tribute. He spoke angrily about the photographers whom he blamed for her death. By his silences also and by oblique hints he displayed his criticism of the royal family. The service was beautiful but did nothing to bring to an end the controversies that surrounded the life of the Princess.

David in his lament for Saul resisted that temptation to be negative and paved the way significantly for the uniting, over time, of the nation of Israel, as we shall see.

TODAY'S CHALLENGES:

Choosing the right subordinates.
The danger of justice deferred.

'[T]he wife of Zebedee came to Jesus with her two sons, bowed before him, and asked him a favour. "What do you want?" Jesus asked her. She answered, "Promise me that these two sons of mine will sit at your right and your left when you are King." "You don't know what you are asking for..."'
(Matt. 20:20-22).

15

The Battle to be Number Two

2 Samuel 1–4

David becoming king of Israel took awhile even after Saul was dead. Naturally, it was a watershed in his career. Embedded in the process were factors that were to become both crucial and very dangerous. One was his domestic arrangements. Six children were born to him in the city of Hebron by six different wives in seven and a half years. We shall return to them and other family members many times in the story (2 Sam. 3:2-5).

The other factor was how he dealt with his number twos. In the story up until now there are hardly any individual names. He did not have an identifiable inner circle. He was a loner, concentrating on surviving well. Now this changed because of the people who wanted to get close to him and the power he wielded. One of them was Abner.

Abner comes into the story as a cousin of King Saul who made him his army commander (1 Sam. 14:50). He was number three in the kingdom next only to Jonathan, Saul's attractive son and heir.

Things changed dramatically for Abner at the battle of Gilboa when Saul and Jonathan were both killed on the same day and the army was routed. What was to happen now? Abner decided to take on himself the role of kingmaker. He assumed that the hereditary principle of succession would apply in Israel although there was no precedent for this. He headed east across the Jordan to Mahanaim, and took an unknown son of Saul, Ishbosheth, and crowned him king over the tribes and towns in the centre and north of the country (2 Sam. 2:8-10). He knew about the prophecy of Samuel about David being destined to be king, but he went ahead anyway (2 Sam. 3:9-10).

In the meantime, news of the defeat of Israel at Gilboa reached David down in the south in Ziklag and he prayed about what he should do. His guidance was to move camp with his men to the city of Hebron and its surrounds. There his fellow tribesmen of Judah anointed him king. His first kingly act was to send warm commendation to the people of Jabesh Gilead, east of the River Jordan, for taking measures to recover the remains of Saul and Jonathan and give them a proper burial.

It must have upset Abner to hear that Judah, the largest tribe both in population and land size, had acted independently and made David king of Judah. Nonetheless, he continued to back Ishbosheth, no doubt as the key to his own power.

Abner, however, had not counted on the ambition of Joab, David's stepsister's son, who himself wanted to be number two in the kingdom. It looks as though these two were sizing each other up. A meeting took place when Abner and other officials of Ishbosheth went south to their tribal territory of Benjamin. Joab and David's officials came up north from Hebron. The two groups sat down on either side of a pool in the city of Gibeon. Abner suggested a tournament, a kind of trial of strength between a group of twelve men from each side. It became clear, however, that both sides saw much more at stake than a friendly joust. The chosen warriors from both sides went in with deadly intent to win at all costs, and all twenty-four were dead within minutes.

This developed into a full scale battle in which Abner slew Asahel, Joab's brother. There followed a two-year war between Judah and the northern tribes. The forces of David eventually began to prevail.

Abner began to realize that he had backed the wrong king. He seized on a petty dispute with Ishbosheth as cause to desert him, and began to propose to David that he bring all Israel over to his side. David agreed and, unknown to Joab, sent Abner to fulfill this mission, which, if achieved would have made Abner number two to David.

When Joab learned what was going on, he promptly had Abner murdered without telling David in spite of the safe passage David had given Abner. This was ostensibly revenge on Abner for killing Joab's brother Asahel, but it was clearly also Joab's pitch to become David's number two. He did it by eliminating his main rival and presented David with a fait accompli.

What was David to do now? The winning of the allegiance of the rest of Israel had not been completed. Abner's assassination would inflame the rest of the country against both David and Judah. It was a very delicate situation. David was furious, even vindictive towards Joab.

He arranged an elaborate funeral for Abner and he himself became the principal mourner. He resorted again to song and composed a poetic lament for Abner as he had for Saul and Jonathan. He spoke out against Joab and his brother and gave a fine eulogy for Abner. It had the desired result. All David's people and all the people in Israel understood that the King had no part in the murder of Abner. 'They took note of this and were pleased. Indeed, everything the king did pleased the people' (2 Sam. 3:36).

I FEEL WEAK TODAY

Then David made a remarkable confession. 'Even though I am the king chosen by God, I feel weak today.' He was weak because of the actions and attitude of his number two. And he was correct. He had lost Abner who was the more experienced of the rivals to become his number two. From the beginning of the struggling new monarchy in Israel, Abner had been right-hand man to the King, gaining experience that no one else had ever had the opportunity to acquire. He had been the one to smooth things over and keep the affairs of state operating when the King's black moods incapacitated him. His military prowess was great and nearly indispensable. He was from Benjamin and his service of David would have helped to bind David's people with Saul's people. And the influence he commanded with the leaders of so many tribes was all gone now that he was dead. It would take years to replace the loss. His assassination left a great gap.

Abner obviously had the maturity to know that killing led to more revenge killing. When Asahel was pursuing Abner after the battle at Gibeon, Abner tried to get him to give up the chase. 'Stop chasing me! Why force me to kill you? How could I face your brother Joab?' Later when Joab and his men were still bent on pursuing Abner's men to the death, Abner called out to Joab, 'Do we have to go on fighting for ever? Can't you see that in the end there will be nothing but bitterness? We are your fellow-countrymen. How long will it be before you order your men to stop chasing us?' (2 Sam. 2:22, 26). Losing that kind of moderation made David weaker. Admitting it helped him with the people at the time. This loss, however, would continue to plague David throughout his life.

POISONED SPRINGS

'These sons of Zeruiah are too violent for me,' David asserted (2 Sam. 3:39). It was the custom in Israel to identify people by linking them with their fathers. David was the son of Jesse. His mother is never named. He himself refers to her only as the handmaiden of the LORD or a godly woman. Very frequently, however, if Joab or either of his brothers Asahel or Abishai are mentioned, they are described as the sons of Zeruiah. The impression is of a mother with a strong personality and a consuming ambition for her sons. She was step-sister to David and he was on the way to the throne. There was ample leverage for her schemes to be pursued, and Joab was her main instrument. It meant, however, that David contended constantly with an alternative agenda and a totally different outlook on life in opposition to what he was himself trying to do. Joab was ruthless, whereas David wanted always to be conciliatory. Joab was scheming, where David tried to be open and direct. Joab was domineering and self-serving, in contrast to David's desire to be the servant of God and of his people. Because they grew up together David knew all this, yet to the end he did not have the will to deal with Joab.

The most David could rise to in the face of Abner's assassination was a very colourful curse: 'May the punishment for it fall on Joab and all his family! In every generation may there be some man in his family who has gonorrhoea or a dreaded skin disease or is fit only to do a woman's work or is killed in battle or hasn't enough to eat!' (2 Sam. 3:29). They were searing, sizzling words, but they left the problem unsolved. A criminal was left unpunished. It would appear that indecision like this was characteristic of David where members of his own family were concerned.

There is no decision a leader can make that is more important than his choice of his number two. By this he makes himself weaker or stronger. It is often the case, as with David, that this post is filled by default. It is a non-choice. It just happens. It can be because of ties of kinship, as here. It can be because of a prior debt. Perhaps the person is just there, a given, and there is not enough sense of will or determination to remove them and bring in someone better.

I heard a talk by David Putnam, the film producer, just after he had made the film, 'Chariots of Fire'. He expressed his own disillusionment with many Number Ones and said, 'It is the Number Twos that make the world go round.'

If proof of that is needed, the creation of the European Economic Community is a good example. Jean Monnet, more than any other, is credited with bringing that institution into being. It is illuminating to know how he did it. Although he knew and was known to all the heads of state in his time, he seldom ever approached them directly. He always worked through their Number Twos, putting proposals to them to be placed before their superiors, often in their own name. He found this the most effective method (*Jean Monnet* by Francois Duchene, pp. 355-356, 1994, Norton, NY).

After Abner's assassination, David just waited. He did not have long to wait. Panic gripped Ishbosheth and his followers. Two of them decided to take matters into their own hands. They assassinated Ishbosheth and took his severed head down to David. David again was shocked and showed it. He executed the assassins and gave Ishbosheth's remains an honoured place in the tomb of Abner. But he overlooked the crime of Joab and left a deadly weakness at the heart of his administration.

Apparently David's immediate actions and words received approval across the country, for not long afterwards all the tribes of Israel came to David at Hebron and said to him, "We are your own flesh and blood. In the past, even when Saul was still our king, you led the people of Israel in battle, and the LORD promised you that you would lead his people and be their ruler." So all the leaders of Israel came to King David at Hebron. He made a sacred alliance with them, they anointed him, and he became king of Israel' (2 Sam. 5:1-3).

TODAY'S CHALLENGE:

Securing broad-enough support.

Jesus said, 'Everyone whom my Father gives me will come to me.
I will never turn away anyone who comes to me, because I have come
down from heaven to do not my own will but the will of him
who sent me.'
(John 6:38)

16
Rule by Consent

2 Samuel 2–5

It is worth pausing to register just how David came to the throne of Israel. After years of being outlawed he became king at the age of thirty over his own tribe, Judah. Some years later he became king over all Israel. In our past consideration of this young man we have seen enough to know that a move like this could go very badly or very well.

PATIENCE THAT SHOWED GREAT MATURITY OF JUDGMENT

David was in advance of his time and certainly ahead of most men of his years in that he seemed to know that some ways of becoming a leader can carry a risk of failure, unless they are corrected. Instinctively, he did the right things to avoid failure.

First, he asked the LORD, "Shall I go and take control of one of the towns of Judah?" "Yes," the LORD answered. "Which one?" David asked. "Hebron," the LORD said.' Only then does he go. When his men have settled in the environs of Hebron, the elders of the people come and ask him to be their king, and so David became king over his own tribe, Judah, by the requests of the representatives of the people (2 Sam. 2:4).

After the death of Abner, two men took it into their hands to slay Ishbosheth, Saul's son, expecting David to become king and reward them. Again he completely disassociated himself from this act of violence. Eventually the representatives of the various tribes come over to David at Hebron. They are 'men expressly named to come and make David king'; 'men who knew what Israel should do and the best time to do it'; 'men who came to help David with singleness of purpose'. All these came to Hebron with full intention to make David king over Israel; likewise the rest of Israel were of like mind to make David king. It was an amazing movement. It was worth waiting seven years to see it. David's military ability and the support that he had earlier meant that he might have secured the rule of the whole country by force of arms. But he waited to be chosen, even though he had been anointed by Samuel. It is summed up in the words, 'David made a sacred alliance with them 'they anointed him, and he became king of Israel' (2 Sam.5:3).

A POLITICAL ARRANGEMENT IN ADVANCE OF ITS TIME

David's action was all the more remarkable when you consider what the neighbouring rulers were like. They were oriental despots where the king was completely autocratic and responsible to no one. What he said was law. In some of the neighbouring countries like Egypt and Assyria there was even a belief in the divinity of the king. In the book of Daniel, people were commanded to worship the image of the king (Dan. 3).

Where did this idea of David arise that he should only become king by the choice of the people? He took his ideas from the Law of God. In Deuteronomy 17, sometimes called the Israel Magna Carta, it was anticipated that the people would want a king one day and provision was made. The wording is quite specific. The people might set a king over them. He had to be one of their own people and one that the

LORD had chosen; he had to follow the Law of God. The whole object of the exercise was that he might not think he was better than his fellow Israelites. It is interesting to see how much of this shines out in David's case. He waited for the people to choose him. Then they told him why he was chosen they said, 'We are your own flesh and blood... even when Saul was still our king, you led the people of Israel in battle, and the LORD promised you that you would lead his people and be their ruler' (2 Sam. 5:1-2). The Law as it was given to Moses is mostly followed in how David became king.

Here is a very early example of a covenantal if not a constitutional monarchy, in which God, the people and the candidate person were all parties. Long before Hobbes and Locke we have a brand of social contract theory of government actually in practice. The people by their common consent call in the ruler to fulfil certain functions for them and they surrender certain liberties to him.

This idea of covenantal monarchy was not always adhered to in later history in Judah or Israel. Yet, the better kings that made a difference in Israel accepted this ideal of a covenant between king and people. It came back either by the choice of the people or at the insistence of some priest or prophet. It happens in the case of Joash (2 Kings 11:17) and of Hezekiah (2 Chron. 29:10). The attitude of prophets like Elijah, Elisha, Isaiah, Jeremiah and Amos to the kings of their time shows that it was part of the prophetic burden that the relationship of the governor to the governed was one that was determined by covenant.

BECOMING A LEADER

People become leaders in different ways.

1. Some are leaders because they volunteered.
2. Some become leaders by force of circumstances: crises arise and they are thrown to the front, they take hold of the situation and others follow them.

3. Some are given leadership because they represent a 'father figure' in the eyes of the others who desire authoritative direction.
4. A leader may be chosen because he obviously excels the others.
5. Sometimes the leader is the choice of the majority.
6. Occasionally the leader is imposed by vested interests of one kind and another.
7. A person can become a leader because within them they have a sense of a divine call.

How a person comes to leadership greatly affects what happens thereafter. David started being a 7 in that list; then he moved to 2 and then to 4. He did not, however, rest on any of these. He was determined only to be the leader by the consent and the choice of the majority of people, as per number 5. It is a very remarkable story, so early in history.

This was important. It was vitally important for the unity of Israel. Had he been impatient and rushed to power, he would not have been king over a united nation. By waiting until all were won over, he was able with their united backing to achieve for them what had never been done before. When Israel made David king, he began to save them from their enemies internally and externally. What a waste it was in Israel the seven-and-a-half years when the country was divided and many were going after Ishbosheth and Abner. We shall see what progress began immediately to take place under the rule of David.

ADDITIONAL NOTE ON THE KINGDOM OF GOD

It would be easy but wrong to read too much into David's role in creating a model of government. He was, however, a significant player in developing the social, aesthetic, political and economic aspects of 'The Kingdom of God'.

I have the impression that when people hear the words, 'The Kingdom of God' in English, they experience the MEGO effect (My Eyes Glaze Over). This is disappointing because the person usually has a sense that the 'The Kingdom of God' is a very important truth. The ambiguity arises, perhaps, because in the Anglo-Saxon world we have not had a king with any real authority for 400 years. The United Kingdom and the Commonwealth have a constitutional monarchy, where the real power is with Parliament and governmental institutions. The USA is a republic with a president and there is something missing in the very idea of 'God's Republic'.

It does not help our understanding when 'The Kingdom of God' bursts on our ears from the lips of Jesus, seemingly without notice at the beginning of his ministry. There is no obvious preparation in the OT for this central theme of Jesus' gospel. The phrase or an equivalent occurs only half a dozen times in the OT. That does not mean that there is no preparation for the theme in the OT. It is the purpose of this note to outline how the whole idea arose, the part David played in its development and how it works out in the rest of the Bible. I shall do this with a few contrasts.

It is 'The Kingdom of God' as Contrasted with the Kingdoms of Man (cf. Rev. 11:15 av)

The most important word in the phrase is 'God'. It really takes us back to, 'In the beginning, when God...' (Gen. 1:1), and it is the God revealed mainly through Abraham and Moses. Way ahead of their time, the people of the OT learned vital things about the nature of God.

- He is the one and only God. There is no other.
- He is the Creator of everything.
- He rules all nature and controls all history.
- He is just, righteous and loving and operates by laws which can be known.
- He is universal, all over the world.
- He is eternal in every age and beyond.

It is this kind of God whose Kingdom it is.

'THE KINGDOM OF GOD' IS ABOUT SOCIETIES AS WELL AS INDIVIDUALS

This is why the concept was processed through the history of the nation state of Israel, beginning with David. God chose a people, Israel, to love and through whom he could reveal himself and his ways. After they became big enough to be a nation, they operated as a theocracy which means the rule of God. There was little or no central government. Each tribe operated on the basis of God's Law as given through Moses and by turning up periodically at a central shrine to worship God. This did not work very well as we see in the book of Judges.

The people decided they needed a king like the other nations. There was provision for this in the Law (Deut. 17:14-20), so they got a king. The first was Saul and he was a failure. They then got David and he was a success. He united the twelve tribes into a nation, defeated their enemies, established their borders, and gave them a capital city and centralized their worship. They began to develop politically, economically, aesthetically, and the name of 'the Kingdom of Israel' rose in the world. This, however, was a long way from being 'the Kingdom of God'.

The united kingdom of Israel lasted only for one more reign, that of Solomon. Then it split again into two kingdoms, Israel and Judah, and in each they had kings that were far from being good kings. The nostalgic dream of again having a king like David was often expressed but it never happened. Indeed, it went from bad to worse and eventually both kingdoms were humiliated and taken into exile.

The dream of having a king like David did not die. It began to be expressed by prophets for a future time, when God would intervene, defeat their enemies and establish his Kingdom with his anointed prince (=Messiah). The debate about this between the rulers, the prophets and the people all through these centuries was about how people should live, good and bad government, and about true and false worship. That debate is the content of the OT.

This leaves us with a background to the concept of the Kingdom of God that is very national and quite political. People in Jesus' day were very conscious of experiencing bad government. When Jesus spoke about the 'The Kingdom of God', they thought in terms of a renewed Kingdom of Israel becoming the Kingdom of God. Even the disciples after the cross and resurrection are still asking, 'Will you at this time restore the kingdom to Israel?' They had not yet grasped what he meant by 'The Kingdom of God'.

It is always a matter of surprise to discover how unevenly the NT uses the concept of 'The Kingdom of God'. Its major use is in Matthew and Luke. It is scarce in Mark and even scarcer in John. Acts has only eight references and there are ten letters in the NT that do not speak of 'The Kingdom of God' at all. What takes its place is what has come to be called, 'The Lordship of Christ'.

The gospel spread in the Roman Empire where the supreme ruler was the emperor who was called *Kurios* or 'Lord'. Talking about kings and kingdoms was not common or helpful. Paul and the early gentile Christians recast the essentially Jewish concept of 'The Kingdom of God' by asserting that Jesus, not the emperor, was Lord. This is the word all through the New Testament. By the time we get to Revelation the two are put side by side. Jesus is 'King of Kings and Lord of Lords'.

Now the concept of emperor does not translate well into modern times either. The result is that when Christians use the words, 'The Lordship of Christ', they seem to make this a very personal statement as it applies to them and their own personal lives. The corporate and social and political overtones of 'The Kingdom of God' are lost.

I recall coming back to the UK just after the Sixties and finding many people who had been brought up in the Christian Brethren and similar groups with an almost exclusive Pauline theology. They had just discovered the Gospels and it revolutionized their outlook. 'The Kingdom of God' became their theme and their application of the gospel widened considerably. It needed to.

'THE KINGDOM OF GOD' IS ABOUT HERE AND NOW AND NOT JUST THE FUTURE

When Jesus came saying 'The Kingdom of God' is at hand, or near, the important word was 'at hand'. Everyone had gone through the process of becoming disillusioned about their government and their societies and were reconciled to thinking that someday, in the sweet by and by, the Kingdom of God would come. Don't ask me when! Don't ask me how! I need to get on with my life and trust God to make it all right in the end. I think many are still at ease with that minimal concept of 'The Kingdom of God'. It is when Jesus will come again and set everything right.

That was what Jesus was getting at. 'The Kingdom of God' is here, now! You do not need to wait until the end. He was saying that the Kingdom was present in himself as its king and that, to all intents and purposes, those who believed this Good News could adopt in this life a way of thinking where they lived their lives subject to God, whatever their government. He had come to achieve this and if they would transfer their allegiance to him from whoever or whatever controlled their thinking, the Kingdom of God would be present for them here and now.

Now that is a tall order. Yet, if God is the God who is described in my first section above, then that becomes possible for he is in control whatever... We can live now in the light of the future triumph of the just, righteous and loving God. The Kingdom is now as well as not yet.

'THE KINGDOM OF GOD' IS ABOUT A PERSON, NOT A SYSTEM OR REGIME

The nation of Israel learned through their bad experience of successive rulers that what they needed was a king like the idealised David that they remembered. People have continued to search in theory and in practice for the ideal form of government. Kingdom, empire, republic, democracy, theocracy, in many forms have all been both advocated and tried and all have been found wanting. Apartheid South Africa thought that it could be a modern example of Israel and inherit the promises given to the people of God. Some have hoped for a British Israel. Language can be heard suggesting that the United States, if it followed the Law of God in the Bible could restore something approximating to the Kingdom of God on earth. Hitler believed that an Aryan world empire could be created and provide a utopia in the twentieth century and beyond. Stalin and Mao Tse Tung thought that a communist state could provide the ideal for people to live and die for. How wrong they were!

Jesus' announcement of 'The Kingdom of God' serves notice that there is no human system or person that will meet human needs in their entirety. Only God can do that and his son Jesus is the one who will bring that about now and in the end. When Jesus said that 'The Kingdom of God' was here now, he was at least serving notice that there could be approximations to the Kingdom of God in this life, if those who believed the good news could live its truths and principles in their own immediate surroundings.

The Kingdom of God is not the Church and the Church is not the Kingdom of God, but each local church can become an outpost of 'The Kingdom of God' in its community modelling the kind of life that is pleasing to God and in its proclamation of the Good News of the Kingdom.

Today's Challenges:

The priority of unity.
The need for symbols of unity.
Appointing people for the wrong reasons.
Who is benefiting from the leadership.

Jesus said, 'I pray that they may all be one.'
(John 17:20-21)

17
Inspired Strategy

2 Samuel 5:6-15; 1 Chronicles 11:1-9

ENTER JERUSALEM

What was the first thing David did as king of all Israel? Leading up to his coronation, his emphasis had been on unity. It did not change, but how he tackled it was a total surprise. There is no indication it had been in his or in anyone's mind before this. He captured and went to live in Jerusalem.

He was still living and held court in the town of Hebron, about twenty miles south of what became Jerusalem. He had reason to know the hill fortress called Jebus from the days when he lived in Bethlehem and herded his father's sheep. Jebus was only about six miles away to the north. It is likely that in looking for water or pasture, or in searching for lost sheep he had come close to this place. It did not belong to Israel. It had never been occupied by them. It had sat there for centuries, sticking out like a defiant sore thumb in the landscape. It looked impregnable with sheer slopes on three sides and only approachable with difficulty from the north.

It had the distinction in the historical record of being one of the places where the Israelites could not drive out the local inhabitants, the Jebusites. The Jebusites were one of the standard list of seven nations – all ending in *–ites* that God was going to drive out in order to give Israel the Promised Land (Deut. 7:1). For some reason David hated the Jebusites (2 Sam. 5:8). Perhaps it was for the patriotic reason that they had resisted capture all these centuries. Perhaps he had been the object of their taunts as a boy when he had to rescue sheep from their foothills.

A FOCUS FOR UNITY

Joshua says it was Judah that could not drive them out (Josh. 15:63). Judges says it was Benjamin that failed (Judg. 1:21). This is not surprising as it was on the border between Judah and Benjamin. It is the genius of David that he saw the value of the place. It did not belong to any tribe. It was fairly central. It had no obvious traditions associated with any of the ancestors, like Hebron, the burial place of Abraham, or Shiloh, where the Ark of the Covenant had been located, or Shechem, where Joshua had addressed the people. It could be a place around which the whole country could unite as they never had done in the past. From the time of the occupation there had been no successful centralization of the state. They were a scattered group of twelve tribes that could be picked off one by one by hostile invaders, as indeed they were picked off repeatedly. Equally they found it difficult to suppress their own tribal rivalries. This place had the potential of becoming a capital of which they could all be proud, like Washington DC in USA or Canberra in Australia. It could be a focus for unity.

This new site could be fortified more easily than any other place in the whole country. It was high and inaccessible because of the steep slopes on three sides. Over the centuries this was proved to be true. Whatever happened in the rest of the country, the seat of government was secure and they could fight back from there, given time.

It still had to be captured, however, before any plans for it could be implemented. It was still impregnable and its people were arrogantly confident that even a garrison of disabled people could hold it against any attackers. David, however, had found its weak spot, perhaps when he was looking for water for his sheep in earlier years. It was a tunnel that gave the city its water supply. He challenged his elite troops to attack it clandestinely via the tunnel. They did and they succeeded.

It is interesting to speculate how the course of the history of Israel might have been changed if Joshua or Caleb, or both had captured the hill of Jebus for Israel at the time of the conquest and not left it as one of the places from which they did not drive out their enemies. Would it have provided the focus for unity among the twelve tribes from the start? Would the depressing cycle of oppression and deliverance recorded in Judges have been avoided? This can only be speculation about one of history's great might-have-beens. In the event it took David with his gifts and sense of calling to detect its value in transforming the tribes into a nation.

A BLUNDER

In the process, David inadvertently compounded the mistake he had made earlier in refusing to discipline his army chief, Joab, for the murder of Abner. With bravado he called out, 'The first man to kill a Jebusite will be commander of the army!' Joab seized the opportunity, got through the tunnel first, slew a Jebusite and established himself as David's Number Two for good or ill. An unreformed criminal was made Prime Minister, Chief of Police and Commander of the Army. Joab had all of these functions. In no time Joab was restoring the rest of the city while David concentrated on his own palace' (1 Chron. 11:8 GNB). This was the beginning of the remarkable architectural history of Jerusalem.

A PLACE OF HIS OWN

David, the homeless outlaw, at last had a home of his own and he lived there. It became known as David's City. For hundreds of years after this in the OT histories, it is referred to as David's City. Now in history, the city has been the strongest force for breaking the tribal mentality. People from many tribes become fellow citizens, with a common language, common interests, common problems. In Jerusalem David created the first city of any significance in Israel. It became the focus of unity for a very divided group of tribes.

THE CITY OF GOD

Strangely, however, Jerusalem is never referred to as David's City in the Psalms whether they are claimed for David or composed by someone else. The circumstances of its capture made everyone think that it was the LORD who had given them the city. 'The LORD built his city on the sacred hill' (Ps. 87:1). It began to be called the City of God. In the Psalms attributed to David he calls Jerusalem by its pre-Israelite name, 'Zion', about a dozen times. When he is in poetic mood, he shows what his real inner thoughts are about this new city of his. It is the LORD who rules in Zion (Ps. 9:11). The LORD is mighty in Zion (Ps. 99:2), and from Zion the LORD can and will extend his power (Ps. 110:2). The historical text at the point of its unexpected capture says that David grew stronger all the time because the LORD was with him. It seems that the very existence of Zion was the final and perpetual evidence to David that he was God's servant in ruling Israel and he was acting for God in doing so. His moments of deepest doubt, depression and despair were when he was driven out of Jerusalem by Absalom, his rebel son, and could not go back to his beloved city.

He also saw Zion a centre from which victory would extend ever more widely (Ps. 14:7). Equally it was and would be a source from which help and aid would come to Israel when it was needed (Ps. 20:2). As a consequence, the people of Zion were glad. It was a happy place of pride and peace (Ps. 97:8). Supremely, however, it was 'Zion, [God's] sacred hill' (Ps. 43:3), where worship was offered to the LORD, and how that developed is the subject of the next chapter.

ZIONISM

Here is the fountainhead of a word and a concept that still resonates throughout the world today. Every Sunday, where Christian hymns are sung in whatever language, Zion is transliterated and lifts the spirits of the worshipper in hope-generating praise.

> Glorious things of thee are spoken,
> Zion, city of our God.
> He whose word cannot be broken
> Formed thee for his own abode.
> Saviour if of Zion's city
> I, through grace a member am,
> Let the world deride or pity,
> I will glory in thy name.

Theologically it has become the battleground in the field of eschatology or the doctrine of the end times. What place has Jerusalem in the purposes of God, today and in the future? This debate has been fuelled by political Zionism and its success since the re-establishment of the State of Israel in 1948 and the capture of Jerusalem in 1967. Zionism takes many forms in the hands of different devotees. None of them would even have been thought of if David had not captured Jerusalem and gone to live there.

FOR THE SAKE OF HIS PEOPLE

There is one further significant note about David introduced at the capture of Jerusalem. 'David realized that the LORD had established him as king of Israel and was making his kingdom prosperous for the sake of his people' (2 Sam. 5:12). David realized that the reason for his success was not his skill or flare. The point of his success was not what it meant to or did for him. The point was what it meant and was going to mean for the people he was to rule. He might be King of Israel, but he was so only under the kingship of the LORD. What the LORD was concerned about was not David's career, however illustrious, but the people and their wellbeing. If he was to be the shepherd of Israel, the shepherd was there for the sheep, not for the shepherd. This becomes a frequent note in the prophets. They saw only too frequently that leaders, however well they began, ended up by being for themselves and not for those they led.

ADDITIONAL NOTE ON THE CITY OF GOD AS A METAPHOR FOR THE CHURCH

It is remarkable that we are one-quarter of the way through the Bible and only now does Jerusalem appear in the story. David wanted it to be the place where God would put his name (Deut. 12:4-7). He brought the Ark of the Covenant there and wanted to build its Temple. He saw it as potentially the City of God. This became an important concept for the understanding of the nature of the Church.

It is sometimes said that the Bible begins in a garden and ends in a city. How did that transition take place? It is a tortuous but fascinating story.

Chapter 1. One of the consequences of the Fall of Man when he was driven out of the Garden was that Cain founded a city, and music and technology had their beginnings (Gen. 4:17-22). Soon in their pride people built Babel, with a tower that reached the sky, so that they could make a name for themselves and not be scattered all over the earth. 'This brought on them the judgment of God. So the LORD scattered them all over the earth, and they stopped building the city. The city was called Babylon.' Babylon became the symbol of the city which was not of God.

Chapter 2. Abram lived in the idolatrous city of Ur of the Chaldees. From there God called him out to an unknown destination. Hebrews tells us that he 'was waiting for the city which God has designed and built, the city with permanent foundations' and implies that he did not find it (Heb. 11:10).

Chapter 3. Centuries later, David captured Jerusalem and made it the centre for the worship of the LORD in the Temple. The phrase 'City of God' was first used in the Psalms, sometimes ecstatically.

> The LORD built his city on the sacred hill; more than any other place in Israel he loves the city of Jerusalem. Listen, city of God, to the wonderful things he says about you: 'I will include Egypt and Babylonia when I list the nations that obey me; I will number among the inhabitants of Jerusalem the people of Philistia, Tyre, and Sudan.' Of Zion it will be said that all nations belong there and that the Almighty will make her strong. The LORD will write a list of the peoples and include them all as citizens of Jerusalem. They dance and sing, 'In Zion is the source of all our blessings' (Ps. 87).

By implication this was the rival to the cities that were not of God.

In time, and ironically, it was the King of Babylon, Nebuchadnezzar, who captured and destroyed Jerusalem in 596 BC and took its people as exiles to Babylon where the contrast could hardly be greater.

> By the rivers of Babylon we sat down; there we wept when we remembered Zion. On the willows near by we hung up our harps. Those who captured us told us to sing; they told us to entertain them: 'Sing us a song about Zion.' How can we sing a song to the LORD in a foreign land? May I never be able to play the harp again if I forget you, Jerusalem! May I never be able to sing again if I do not remember you, if I do not think of you as my greatest joy! (Ps. 137:1-6).

The prophets, however, foretold the destruction of Babylon and the restoration of Jerusalem (Isa. 14; 60:14).

Chapter 4. Again Jerusalem goes out of business. It happens after Jesus is crucified in the city and foretells its destruction which happens in AD70 and AD132 (Luke 21:20-24.)

In this period, a new language begins to be used by the Christians in the NT. They talk about 'the Holy City, the new Jerusalem' (Gal. 4:26; Rev. 21:2), 'the city of the living God, the heavenly Jerusalem' (Heb. 12:22). Christians are calling each other 'fellow-citizens' (Eph. 2:19), 'citizens of heaven' (Phil. 3:20). Jerusalem and the City of God are taking on new meanings.

Add the fact that the word that Jesus and then the apostles use for the Church is the Greek word '*ecclesia.*' The *ecclesia* in the Greek translation of the Old Testament referred to Israel, gathered in solemn assembly as the people of God.

In the Greek world it was the word that had been used since the fifth century for the assembly of citizens. The *ecclesia* in the Greek city state, like Athens, was the assembly of citizens in which decisions were made and laws passed. So, in Greek, this word had political overtones. The way in which Paul suggests that the churches should carry out their business makes it clear that this autonomous decision-making function under Christ was part of its nature (1 Cor. 5:3–6:8).

Another word that is used for the Church is the 'body'. The Church is described as a body with many limbs and organs. Paul says that this is what baptism introduces us to (1 Cor. 12:13). The truths that are important in this picture are:

- Every Christian has some gifts or skills (Eph. 4:7).
- These give each person a role in the community (Rom. 12:6).
- The whole community functions by interdependence (1 Cor. 12:12, 26; Eph. 4:11-16).
- This interdependence works when each is controlled by the head (Col. 2:19; Eph. 4:15, 16).
- Some of the activities are internal to the Church, others are external for the world (Rom. 12:7-8; 1 Cor. 12:4-11, 27-30).

It is significant that for centuries Greek philosophers like Aristotle had applied this image of the body to the state or the body politic. This language was commonplace in Greece.[1]

This would seem to imply that Paul sees the Church as a potential microcosm of what the society at large should be – a city within their city. If the Church saw itself this way it would model, in its harmonious and forgiving relationships and in the efficient way it which it conducts its business, the ideals that God has for corporate life. This would be a useful corrective of the tendency to use this image of the Church in too pietistic way.

Chapter 5. Has still to happen. It is described in the book of Revelation. Babylon, the city which is not of God, is dramatically destroyed (Rev. 18). Then is inaugurated the Holy City, the new Jerusalem, coming down out of heaven from God. John heard a loud voice speaking from the throne: 'Now God's home is with mankind! He will live with them, and they shall be his people. God himself will be with them, and he will be their God.' There would be no need of a Temple in this city (Rev. 21:2-3, 22).

---

1. See Coriolanus Act 1, scene 1 for an example in English of this metaphor from the classical period.

TODAY'S CHALLENGES:

Learning from mistakes.
Doing the right things and doing
things right.
A spouse that does not understand.

'My son, pay attention when the Lord corrects you, and do not be discouraged when he rebukes you. Because the Lord corrects everyone he loves, and punishes everyone he accepts as a son.'
(Heb. 12:5-6)

18
Trying to Use God

2 Samuel 6:1-23; 1 Chronicles 13:1-14; 15:25–16:6

THE ARK OF THE COVENANT

David and Joab began building out Jerusalem to make it larger, more habitable and more defensible. In fact, Jerusalem became a building site for some years. While this was going on, David had a idea. He remembered the Ark of the Covenant that was sitting neglected about ten miles to the west of their busy new capital city (1 Chron. 13:3). He thought he would bring the Ark in to Jerusalem with great ceremony.

The Ark of the Covenant was an ancient, valuable, much revered and very sacred item of ecclesiastical furniture. Its design came from God through Moses and it was made by skilled craftsmen (Exod. 25:10-22). It was basically an elaborate chest, full of significant symbols. It was not large (4' x 2.5' x 2.5'). Arching up from a solid gold lid called the mercy seat were two winged angelic figures facing each other. Inside the box were the tablets on which were written the Ten Commandments and some other historic artefacts. It was central to the way that Israel worshipped God. It was also a symbol of the fountainhead of their morality, containing, as it did, the Ten

Commandments. The LORD was a God with the character and values that made the Ten Commandments mandatory on those who would worship him.

Historically it symbolized the presence of God. When the Israelite camp moved, it went in front, carried, on two poles through rings on the side, by designated priests. It preceded the people when they crossed the River Jordan into the Promised Land. It played a part in the capture of Jericho, the first city to fall to the Israelite invaders. It became the centrepiece of a place to worship God at a town called Shiloh (Josh. 3, 6, 18).

The only negative story about the Ark took place about half a century before David. The army used it as a kind of talisman to try and reverse a defeat in war which they had brought on themselves. It did not work. They were totally routed a second time, the shrine at Shiloh was destroyed and the Ark was captured by the Philistine enemy. It was a clear sign that they could not use God to suit their convenience. After a series of drastic mishaps the Ark was returned in a new ox-drawn cart and stayed in obscurity at the home of Abinadab about ten miles west of Jerusalem (1 Sam. 4–7:1).

The Ark did not belong to any one tribe. This may have been why it had been neglected. Now that David had united all Israel it seemed appropriate to bring this national symbol into the new capital city. David planned a mass event. He called in all of his 30,000 soldiers from all over the country to augment the crowds of people who lived nearby. The Ark was mounted on another new cart and drawn by oxen along the hilly road towards the new citadel.

A PROCESSION GONE WRONG

It did not go well. 'David and all the Israelites were dancing and singing with all their might to honour the LORD. They were playing harps, lyres, drums, rattles, and cymbals.' It was an atmosphere of euphoria and sacred dancing bordering on hysteria. Then there was a tragic accident. One of the priest's sons thought that the Ark was going to fall off the cart, and he put a hand out to steady it and dropped dead. The way the story is told, it is clear that David and everyone else thought it was a divine judgment because the Ark had been improperly handled. Everything came to a standstill. The Ark was pushed into the nearest house and the great crowd dispersed sadly to their homes, near and far. One of David's dreams had ended in a nightmare.

David was first angry and then scared before God, no doubt about the death of the priest and the disruption of his precious and very public plans. This was not a new or unusual experience for David. There are several Psalms where he shows that he wrestled with the same emotional reactions. He wrote in Psalm 6, 'LORD, don't be angry and rebuke me! Don't punish me in your anger! I am worn out, O LORD; have pity on me! Give me strength; I am completely exhausted and my whole being is deeply troubled.' It was a fairly frequent dialogue that he had with God as several psalms show.

In this instance, we do not know how his thinking went. From what follows, however, it looks as though he went back to the drawing board and looked again at his actions and the history of the Ark. I imagine some of those who remembered the destruction of Shiloh recounted that experience and drew out the lesson that the Ark was not an item anyone could appropriate for his own purposes. Anyway, he came out with new resolve.

A SECOND ATTEMPT

First, he and others noted that it was not the Ark itself that had been the problem. In fact, a noticeable blessing came on the man and his family where the Ark had been hurriedly parked. So the problem must have been in the way it was handled.

This is evident in the changes that took place when David reinstated the transfer of the Ark three months later. He prepared a tent in which the Ark might be housed. It was carried by hand in the prescribed manner and not hauled on a cart. Then there were Levites, or assistant priests, on hand, duly prepared to do the thing properly

(1 Chron. 16:1-6). The whole event was preceded by a sacrifice to God and has the feel of being much more regulated.

The crowds were there again and there was more merrymaking and ecstatic sacred dance before the Lord. David himself danced before the Ark with abandon until it was lodged in the tent he had prepared. This time he was able to dismiss the crowd in a happier mood. He distributed food to them all. He gave each man and woman in Israel a loaf of bread, a piece of roasted meat and some raisins. Then everyone went home happy.

I had an interesting experience of this story being applied when I was in Africa. I was involved in the east African revival and shared both in their small fellowships and large conventions. There was ecstasy and dancing there from time to time. In the 1960s the Pentecostal churches and the charismatic movement had been spreading and affecting some of 'the brethren' with speaking in tongues and other excessively ecstatic manifestations. I asked William Nagenda, who had been in the revival from its beginning in Rwanda, what the attitude of the leadership was to these new movements. He said, 'Brother Tom, there is no need for us to steady the Ark!'

ONE UNHAPPY LADY

One person was not happy on this colourful day. David's wife Michal was not at all happy. She had, from her window, seen her husband dancing with abandon, half naked before the Ark. She did not approve. She accosted David about it. It was unbecoming for a king. Obviously this was a side of David that she had not known about. David was unbending. He said he had acted as he had to honour the LORD. No doubt he was ecstatic that the Ark was now safely in his new city. It was a dream fulfilled. It was a sign of the LORD's favour.

Michal must have been aware of the habit of the people to sing and dance with abandon when there was occasion to do so. She had surely seen the women sing and dance in honour of her father, Saul, and David after the routing of the Philistines in the battle with Goliath (1 Sam. 18:6-7).

She could not have been unaware of her father Saul's participation in the ecstatic worship in the school of the prophets at the beginning and towards the end of his reign (1 Sam. 10:10-13; 19:18-24). We do not know the story behind her resentment of David's behaviour. We do know that she had a household idol in the house when she used it to help David to escape from the men sent to kill him (1 Sam. 19:13).

It certainly was not inconsistent with David's character. She knew about his music from his harp-playing to soothe her father's dark moods. She heard of his poetry from the laments he composed for Saul and Jonathan and Abner, their commander. The Psalms confirm to us that David's right brain was a great part of him. He was a passionate man. He was forever writing psalms and exhorting others to sing to the LORD, often to shout and sometimes to dance.

Michal, it would seem, had two lines of motivation for her displeasure. First, she felt and said that it was just a PR stunt. The King of Israel was making a big name for himself (2 Sam. 6:20). She might well have been right. The disastrous first attempt to bring in the Ark to the city demonstrated that she was not far from the truth on that occasion. Ironically it was not the name he was making for himself that bothered her. It was the kind of name he was making, a common wifely concern. She would have been happy with a more decorous and sober name fit for his new kingly status and fit for one married to the daughter of King Saul.

The second thing that annoyed her was his exposing of himself and the obvious popularity it won from other women. Again she had a point. The rules required that the priests, when they officiated, should not inadvertently expose themselves (Exod. 20:26 GNB). There was also jealousy there. All that the historian says is that Michal, Saul's daughter, never had any children. She was the only one of his many wives of which this was true. We do not know what was behind this. She had really loved him once (1 Sam. 18:20). She was his first wife. They had been separated for years and she had been married to another man at her father's insistence. Was she barren or did they never really get together again? Whatever it was, her fastidiousness blinded her to something that was of great value to David. In part of a psalm he describes how much it meant to him.

> LORD, do not forget David and all the hardships he endured. Remember, LORD, what he promised, the vow he made to you, the Mighty God of Jacob: "I will not go home or go to bed; I will not rest or sleep, until I provide a place for the LORD, a home for the Mighty God of Jacob." In Bethlehem we heard about the Covenant Box, and we found it in the fields of Jearim. We said, "Let us go to the LORD's house; let us worship before his throne." Come to the Temple, LORD, with the Covenant Box, the symbol of your power, and stay here for ever. May your priests do always what is right; may your people shout for joy!'

MOUNT ZION AND MOUNT SINAI

David wanted Jerusalem to be not just the City of David, but the City of God. That would mean a great deal to David and ultimately to his people. It linked Mount Zion to Mount Sinai and the giving of the Law. Jerusalem succeeds Sinai as a symbol of Israel's status as the special people of God. It made David the successor to Moses after centuries of trouble and chaos. It symbolized that the kingdom of Israel that he would rule would be under God and based on the law enshrined in the Ten Commandments in the Ark. God had promised Moses that he would choose a place for the Ark to dwell where the people could come and worship (Deut. 12:5). David dared to believe that it might be Jerusalem.

TODAY'S CHALLENGES:

Letting fantasies go.
Finding a better reality.

Jesus said, 'the leader must be like the servant."
(Luke 22:26)

19
Beyond His Wildest Dreams

2 Samuel 7

NEVER HAD IT SO GOOD

Everything was going well for David. The whole nation was behind him. He had set up a new capital and brought the Ark of the Covenant into it with great rejoicing. He was living in his own palace in luxury he had never known. He was winning his battles. He was on a roll. He thought about God. He said, 'Here I am living in a house built of cedar, but the Ark of God is kept in a tent!' He would not do less for God than he did for himself. He summoned a prophet called Nathan and shared his concern.

DANGEROUS ADVICE

Nathan said, 'Do whatever you have in mind, because the LORD is with you.' It was hardly surprising. The way things had been going for David it must have seemed to Nathan that his King could walk on water. Everything he touched seemed to prosper and it was obvious that God was with him. So, without thinking, he said, 'Go ahead!' Neither of them prayed or sought God's guidance by any of the means open to them. It is a common mistake to make, but the time when everything is going well is when there is need to take care. You cannot presume on God's blessing if you go and make the decisions. Success in one field does not make you a master in another.

A STEP TOO FAR

Fortunately, Nathan was still sensitive to God and in the night heard God giving him a speech he was to make to David in God's name. It was quite a message. It starts with a question to make David think, a rhetorical question expecting the answer 'No!' 'Are you the one to build me a house to dwell in?' This was not a direct negative. It was an invitation to think and it was followed by the facts that might inform his thinking. Later, David indicated that he felt God was alluding to the fact that he had killed too many people, fought too many wars and caused too much bloodshed (1 Chron. 22:8).

THE INSIDE STORY

At this time, however, Nathan retells Israel's history on this point. 'From the time I rescued the people of Israel from Egypt until now, I have never lived in a temple; I have travelled round living in a tent.' Egypt was famous for its great temples. Although Moses was skilled in all the wisdom of the Egyptians, one that he was not called to use for Israel was the skill of building temples. In other words, God said that this idea of a temple had never come from him. 'I have chosen a place for my people Israel and have settled them there, where they will live without being oppressed any more. Ever since they entered this land, they have been attacked by violent people, but this will not happen again.' It is implied that a temple would not make much difference to this pattern. In fact, there is a distinct impression that a Temple might not necessarily be a good thing. In the light of its later history it was important that this caution should be expressed at the beginning of the project.

There was, however, some good news. God did not dismiss David's idea out of hand. Solomon quotes his father as saying that the message he got was, 'you did well to have this in your heart' (1 Kings 8:18NIV). God credited him with a good intention. God does notice our intentions and commends them even if he does not let us fulfil them. One of David's sons, not yet named, would in fact build a temple for God.

Then there is also a summary of David's past life and future prospects with very great emphasis on the fact that all the initiative was and will be the LORD's. The first person pronoun, 'I', is used seventeen times in telling the national and David's personal story. His future role in God's plan was not different. God outlines what he would do, not what David would achieve. And it was a big surprise.

SOME BETTER THING

God promised him that he would be the beginning of a dynasty in a kingdom that would last forever. 'When you die and are buried with your ancestors, I will make one of your sons king and will keep his kingdom strong. He will be the one to build a temple for me, and I will make sure that his dynasty continues for ever. I will be his father, and he will be my son… You will always have descendants, and I will make your kingdom last for ever. Your dynasty will never end.'

Neither Saul nor David became king because they were sons of a previous king. The idea of having a king at all was new to Israel. We get the distinct impression that it was not the best decision that they had ever made. Up to this point they had only one King, Saul, and he was a failure. Saul wanted his son to become king but it was not to be. David was chosen because he had the gifts and abilities, character, and the spirituality that fitted him for the task. To all intents and purposes, it was a continuation of the situation in the book of Judges. Leaders who had charisma, who had the Spirit of God upon them, were chosen as leaders for a limited period. Saul and David both came to power in this way.

Now God was making a very significant change. Charisma gave way to dynasty. Charisma would never again select a leader in Jerusalem. The leader designated by the Spirit of God had given way to the anointed son of the anointed king. There were always to be descendants of David on the throne of Israel.

This was the hereditary principle. It does not always work in practice. In the the UK there is a running debate about the royal family. Many feel that we should become a republic with an elected head of state. Here we have God instituting the heredity principle and much heresy has been built upon it. Britain suffered in the early 1600s from the idea of the Stuarts that there was a divine right of kings that no one had a right to question.

It is clear, however, that this was not a blank cheque for monarchs. Accountability is built in. God anticipated that it would not go smoothly. 'When he does wrong, I will punish him as a father punishes his son' (2 Sam. 7:14). The history of Israel shows that God kept his word. Eventually, this dynasty became so bad that it ended. The promise of God went underground like some rivers do. Centuries later it surfaced again in Jesus who was King David's greater son. The people clearly had this in mind on Palm Sunday when they welcomed Jesus into Jerusalem. 'Hosanna to the Son of David!' (Mark 11:10). Although no one knew it at the time of David, this promise was the seed out of which came the whole idea of the Kingdom of God preached by Jesus for the whole world.

THE SERVANT LEADER

How did David react to the spoiling of his plans to build a Temple? It is not easy to give up on bright ideas. David's later actions with regard to the Temple his son would build show that he felt this was worthy of the best thought and planning (1 Chron. 22–29).

For the present, however, he was overwhelmed. He went into the Tent where the Ark of God was and sat down and prayed. It is the only time in the Bible that a person is said to have sat down and prayed.

The usual postures were standing, kneeling or prostrating. The words that follow show that David could hardly believe what he had been told. He enthuses over the promise of the dynasty with language that almost seems obsequious. He describes himself as God's 'servant' no less than ten times in as many verses. This is remarkable because he seldom speaks like this anywhere else in the historical text and very few other people call him the servant of God until he is dead. He does call himself God's servant frequently in the Psalms. This is clearly his inner posture and it emerges here because of the momentous nature of what God had told him.

Consider how far he had come from the seemingly unwanted boy left out watching sheep when important things were happening in the house. It is nearly 'From Rags to Riches'. It is no wonder that he was overwhelmed when he counted his blessings.

TODAY'S CHALLENGE:

Inspiring people.

Paul said, 'Do your best to win full approval in God's sight,
as a worker who is not ashamed of his work'.
(2 Tim. 2:15)

20

The Peak of David's Career

2 Samuel 8; 1 Chronicles 18;
2 Samuel 10; 1 Chronicles 19;
2 Samuel 23; 1 Chronicles 11

The peak of David's career was described like this, 'David ruled over all Israel and made sure that his people were always treated fairly and justly' (2 Sam. 8:15). After waiting so many years, David finally had the opportunity to use his leadership abilities to administer the new nation of Israel. When he came to the throne he found no effective administrative structure, only a group of loosely connected tribes with no cohesive life. Some movement toward national unity had occurred under Samuel and Saul, but there had been no really sustained effort. In administering Israel he was doing something for the first time. Here David serves as an example of the effective administrator. In this he followed Moses and took his cue from the books of the Law. There Moses, at the founding of the nation, at great length outlined the organization needed to get the people through the wilderness and into the Promised Land. Now David again illustrates the importance of organization when, for the first time, they occupied all the territory promised to them.

We have noted how he fostered internal unity by winning the voluntary support of all the tribes. Then he captured and created a new and growing capital city in Jerusalem. He also centred the nation's worship in the city by locating the Ark of the Covenant there.

FOREIGN POLICY

His next task was to secure Israel's borders. By successive military conquests he surrounded Israel with a ring of subservient states: on the east Moab and Ammon, on the south the Ammorites and the Philistines, on the north the Arameans and Syrians. In each conquered state he placed garrisons of soldiers, appointed governors, and wherever possible he levied taxes, drew up treaties and made trade pacts. Not only did tribute from these territories fill his treasury, but this series of buffer states also acted as a cushion between Israel and its greater enemies like Egypt to the south and Assyria to the east.

THE MILITARY

The structure of David's army was shaped like a pyramid, with his commander-in-chief, Joab, at the top. Next came a group of men of outstanding ability in the art of war known as The Three, followed by a larger group of distinguished soldiers known as The Thirty. A total of thirty-seven fighting men earned a coveted place in this select group, but their achievements are all played down in comparison to the daring feats of The Three. Underneath these famous fighting men David had an army able to be mobilized from all the people of Israel which he had divided into companies of 1,000 and units of 100 (1 Chron. 13:1). Distinct from this national army, David also maintained a personal bodyguard comprised of Cherethites and Pelethites, probably Aegean peoples, who had very little connection with the mainland of Palestine (2 Sam. 8:18). This independent unit of highly trained men was untouched by tribal rivalries and remained loyal to David even when he was later faced with Absalom's revolution.

ADMINISTRATIVE DISTRICTS

For civil administration David devised a system to smooth the transition from tribe to nation. He divided the country according to population into twelve geographical units from which he expected each month a different group of 24,000 men to be assigned to government service. He retained representatives from the clans and tribes (1 Chron. 27:2-22). Whenever an important matter demanded discussion, both the officers of his new administrative units and the old leaders of the tribes would be heard. David recognized the tribe and the tribal leaders, but he recognized too the need for moving from tribal to national administration.

A CIVIL SERVICE

There was also an embryonic civil service. A minister of finance was responsible for the royal treasury and its tribute money collected from surrounding nations. A deputy finance minister oversaw the collection of taxes from the cities, towns and villages. Under the minister of agriculture one had charge of the vineyards, another of olive and sycamore growing, and a third of the production of olive oil and other products. In the department of animal husbandry David assigned one official to oversee the raising of cattle and camels, another for asses, and a third for sheep and goats (1 Chron. 27:25-31). A minister of works, Adoniram, was responsible for the forced labour of prisoners of war in the construction of public buildings and roads (2 Sam. 20:24). For an emerging nation it made an effective civil service.

To head his administration David formed a cabinet consisting of:

- Joab, the commander-in-chief of the army
- Benaiah, the leader of the bodyguard;
- Two priests, Zadok and Ahimelech, who had belonged to his company for many years

161

- A recorder called Ahilud, who, following the Egyptian administrative model, kept the records, arranged the King's appointments and served as an officer of public relations
- A secretary, who may have been an Egyptian brought in to help organize the palace
- Adoniram, the minister of works; Ahithophel, called the king's counsellor
- and two personal advisors Hushai the Archite, called simply the king's friend

These nine people helped David to move Israel to nationhood (2 Sam. 8:15-18; 20:23-25).

HIS ETHICS

In addition to the historical text, David also wrote an exuberant psalm when the Lord had saved him from Saul and his other enemies (2 Sam. 22:1-51). It is also in Psalm 18, without reservation and in a fulsome way he attributes all his successes, deliverances and accomplishments to God. Sometimes God used the weather in his favour and through it all he attributes even his training and his expertise to God.

The middle section of the psalm sounds somewhat self-righteous to modern Christian ears.

'The LORD rewards me because I do what is right; he blesses me because I am innocent. I have obeyed the law of the LORD; I have not turned away from my God. I have observed all his laws; I have not disobeyed his commands. He knows that I am faultless, that I have kept myself from doing wrong. And so he rewards me because I do what is right, because he knows that I am innocent.

O LORD, you are faithful to those who are faithful to you, and completely good to those who are perfect. You are pure to those who are pure, but hostile to those who are wicked. You save those who are humble, but you humble those who are proud (2 Sam. 22:21-28).

Self-righteous or not, it has the effect, however, of revealing his ethics and the principles by which he sought to rule. Even the self-righteous parts read less bombastically if you use 'when' instead of 'because' and think of him talking about the times when he did, in fact, get it right, which we know and he knew was not every time. There is little doubt that his guiding principle was the Law of the LORD (v. 23) and his goal was justice and fairness for his people.

What made David's administration work?

HE VALUED ABILITY

From the very beginning he rewarded ability. Without regard for tribe or place of origin, he looked for men of ability and gave them responsibility over specific areas of the nation's life. Although David's own tribe of Judah comprised about 25 per cent of the total population, David did not give it preferential treatment. Out of thirty men chosen as leaders of his administration, only seven were known to be from Judah. Among the officers of the twelve administrative districts five came from Judah but others came from Ephraim, from Dan, from Naphtali, from Reuben, from Gilead and from the rival tribe of Benjamin. In fact, in the list of the officers of David's administration nearly all are described by their town of origin rather than by their father's name or by their tribe. The inferences are that David scoured the country for ability and that it didn't matter where he found it. Even if a hamlet didn't merit mention on the map, if he found there a person of demonstrated worth, David would press him into his service.

HE SHOWED APPRECIATION

In the long lists of names of officials in his administration many little details show that David noticed what his men did and who they were. If there was anything to be said to the credit of a man, the recorder inserted it in the text. We know the daring exploits of The Three and many of those of The Thirty (1 Chron. 11). In the lists of men that came to David just before he was made king of Israel, many little phrases light up the narrative with David's appreciation. Men from Judah are described as 'well-equipped men, armed with shields and spears'; men from Simeon are 'well-trained'; men from Zebulun are 'loyal and reliable men ready to fight, trained to use all kinds of weapons'; leaders from Issachar 'knew what Israel should do and the best time to do it'; even men from Ephraim, apparently untested yet in battle, are described as 'men famous in their own clans' (1 Chron. 12). If David could find anything distinctive to say, he made sure that the recorder wrote it down. He fostered loyalty by commending all the qualities that they brought to his service.

HE WAS APPROACHABLE

David's administration succeeded, too, because he was approachable, with some exceptions which his son Absalom was able to exploit (2 Sam. 13:21ff.). Although he headed a growing organization, people could still approach him and have their complaints heard. Nathan could approach him about Bathsheba (2 Sam. 12); the woman of Tekoa sent by Joab could approach him about Absalom (2 Sam. 14). David personally heard cases that were referred to him from the local courts. David himself consulted people. Before he moved the Ark of the Covenant into Jerusalem, 'King David consulted with all the officers in command of units of a thousand men and units of a hundred men. Then he announced to all the people of Israel, 'If you give your approval and if it is the will of the LORD our God, let us send messengers to the rest of our countrymen and to the priests and Levites in their towns, and tell them to assemble here with us. The assembled people discussed his proposal, 'were pleased with the suggestion and agreed to it' (1 Chron. 13:1-4). It was not government for the sake of government, but government for the people. 'David realized that the LORD had established him as king of Israel and was making his kingdom prosperous for the sake of his people' (1 Chron. 14:2).

HE WAS ADAPTABLE

To crown all, David was adaptable. He could change his mind, and he could admit that he was wrong. We saw that in the case of Nabal in Chapter 10.

HE HELD HIMSELF ACCOUNTABLE

He was conscious of having been placed on his throne by God and he held himself accountable to him. This will appear in the rest of the story but it needs to be mentioned here as one of the secrets of his successful leadership.

TODAY'S CHALLENGES:

Marital fidelity.
Not getting others to do our dirty work.
Covering up or owning up?
Not compromising your integrity.

'You will never succeed in life if you try to hide your sins.
Confess them and give them up;
then God will show mercy to you.'
(Prov. 28:13)

21
Almost Gone!

2 Samuel 10–12; Psalms 32 and 51

Normally David led his troops when he went out on a campaign. Then there was an exception. The Ammonites in the east greatly insulted Israel. For the first time David sent Joab with the whole army to deal with the situation, while he remained in Jerusalem. The result was inconclusive. Rabbah, the Ammonite capital, remained in hostile hands and the Syrians were allowed to retreat. David intervened and decisively subdued the Syrians, leaving Rabbah as probably the last pocket of resistance to David's rule. For the second time David sent Joab and the army to deal with it and he again stayed in Jerusalem.

AT A LOOSE END IN JERUSALEM

I am not sure that Jerusalem was always a good thing for David. There is no doubt David longed to get back to it as a place of worship, whenever he was away. Domestic bliss, however, continually eluded him in his own precious city. It was when he sent Joab out the second time, and he remained in Jerusalem, that this sad saga began. It raises the question as to what other things you need to do if you delegate to others what you formerly did yourself. David was left with time on his hands. We do not know who else was in the palace at this time. We do know that he was not short of wives and children and had some concubines (2 Sam. 3:2-4; 5:13-15). Whether they were all housed in Jerusalem we are not told. In any case he was ignoring one of the qualifications that Moses had said a king of Israel should have. He should not 'have many wives' because this would, make him turn away from the LORD' (Deut. 17:17). He seems to have been a pretty red-blooded polygamous male and this is what got him mixed up with Bathsheba when he stayed home in Jerusalem. He spotted her bathing from a rooftop near the palace and she was very beautiful. He found out who she was and then summoned her to the palace and slept with her. She became pregnant and told David. He had committed adultery in private. Now it was going to become public. He decided on a cover-up.

A COVER-UP

Plan A was to call Bathsheba's husband, Uriah, home from the front and make it look as though he was the father of the child. Uriah foiled this plan. He would not go home to his wife. He stayed in the barracks.

Plan B was to organize Uriah's death on the battle field, so that Bathsheba could be protected from stoning and David could then marry her. He was determined not to own up. He would cover up at all costs. He gave the task to Joab his commander, in sealed instructions which Uriah carried with him to the siege of Rabbah. Joab complied, and Uriah and several others were killed in a skirmish in the siege of the city. David married Bathsheba. The cover seemed to have worked and we assume that few people were any the wiser. Life reverted to normal, or so it seemed for a year or so while Bathsheba carried and gave birth to the child and began to bring it up.

It was remarkable that David should have felt the need to go through this elaborate routine to cover his tracks. The kings of neighbouring countries and empires were autocratic despots, often regarded as divine. They could do as they pleased and they did. They took whatever women they wanted and had the power of life and death over their subjects and especially their soldiers. If the people wanted a king like the other nations (1 Sam. 8:5) then they were surely getting it in this respect with David. David's own discomfort with what he had done had its explanation in the values of Israel from ancient times. He had said in his recent psalm of triumph, 'I have obeyed the law of the LORD; I have not turned away from my God. I have observed all his laws; I have not disobeyed his commands' (2 Sam. 22:22-23). One of the Laws was 'You shall not commit adultery'.

A PARABLE

These values were reinforced for David. '[T]he LORD was not displeased with what David had done. The LORD sent the prophet Nathan to David' (2 Sam. 11:27–12:1). He told a parable. 'There were two men who lived in the same town; one was rich and the other poor. The rich man had many cattle and sheep, while the poor man had only one lamb, which he had bought. He took care of it, and it grew up in his home with his children. He would feed it with some of his own food, let it drink from his cup, and hold it in his lap. The lamb was like a daughter to him. One day a visitor arrived at the rich man's home. The rich man didn't want to kill one of his own animals to prepare a meal for him; instead, he took the poor man's lamb and cooked a meal for his guest.'

'David was very angry with the rich man and said, "I swear by the living LORD that the man who did this ought to die! For having done such a cruel thing, he must pay back four times as much as he took." Very pious! Very commendable! Except that Nathan interrupted with deadly accuracy, 'You are that man'. The cover-up was blown. Nathan had used a truth that is often not recognized. If you can criticise something, then you are showing that you know the rule and cannot be surprised if it is applied to you.

OWNING UP

David does not argue or get angry. He says, 'I have sinned against the LORD'. This, however, is about more than the exposure of an instance of adultery and multiple murder. Here is an experience of deep moral significance, which, when linked with Psalms 32 and 51 that were written afterwards is timeless in its reference.

If we put the factual account together with the parable and denunciation of Nathan, then we can chart the progress of David's soul through his deepest fall and perhaps his most sublime recovery.

WHAT SIN IS

Over that terrible year David learned the essential nature of sin. Not content with seven wives, David had robbed Uriah of his only wife.

Sin involves taking what belongs to another. Breaking the first commandment, to have no other gods robs God of his place; the second, not to make graven images, robs God of his character; the third, about taking the name of God in vain robs God of his due respect; the fourth commandment, about the Sabbath Day robs God of his worship; the fifth, about parents robs them of their maintenance and respect; the sixth, about killing robs men of their lives; the eighth, about stealing robs men of their property; the ninth, about false witness robs men of their good name and character; the tenth, about coveting takes away all these things in intent rather than in the act.

- *Sin is to lack pity* (2 Sam. 12:6). David said that the rich man in the parable had no pity for the poor man. He failed to put himself sympathetically in the place of the other who was affected by his action. Then Nathan revealed that David was in fact describing his own lack of pity for Uriah.

- *Sin is to lack a sense of proportion* (vv. 2-3). It values the present moment rather than the longer consequences.

- *Sin is to lack gratitude for what you have* (vv. 7, 8). Nathan continued, this is what the Lord God of Israel says: "I made you king of Israel and rescued you from Saul. I gave you his kingdom and his wives; I made you king over Israel and Judah. If this had not been enough, I would have given you twice as much. Why, then, have you disobeyed my commands?" (2 Sam. 12:7-9). In one night David forgot all that life had already given him, and all that God was yet to give him. He failed to be grateful for what he had or realize what he would lose. His whole perspective was momentarily warped.

- *Sin despises God and his Law* (vv. 9, 10, 14). David had ignored God's Word. Maybe he thought he would be an exception to the rule. Maybe he thought God would turn a blind eye. Maybe he thought God did not understand the difficult conditions in his household. Nathan called this attitude by its true name, contempt for the Almighty.

WHAT NOT TO DO WITH SIN

In the long, dismal year when David tried to ignore his sin, he learned what not to do in such a case.

- *Cover up wrongdoing by stepping up righteousness in other areas.* He tried to treat Uriah generously, granting him leave from the army, entertaining him with royal hospitality and urging him to go home to his wife. He also tried to compensate for his private wrongdoing by his strictness as a judge of public wrongdoing. David meted out justice with unerring perception when people came to him with their unresolved quarrels. When Nathan came to him with his story of the rich man and the poor man, David exploded with characteristic anger against the rich man: 'I swear by the living LORD that the man who did this ought to die! For having done such a cruel thing, he must pay back four times as much as he took' (2 Sam. 12:5-6). David, however, was just compensating for his own guilt, attempting to direct attention away from himself onto the weaknesses of others.

- *Remove one sin by another.* It was worse than useless to try and remove the first sin by committing another. He tried to cover up his adultery first by deceit and then by murder. He discovered, to his consternation, that the piling of sin upon sin, once begun, could multiply exponentially until it got out of control.

- *Delay dealing with it.* He delayed for the best part of a year and had to say, 'When I did not confess my sins, I was worn out from crying all day long. Day and night you punished me, LORD; my strength was completely drained, as moisture is dried up by the summer heat' (Ps. 32:3-4). Sin took its toll on David and his capacity to govern.

- *Implicate another in his sin and put himself in the other's power.* David's desperate decision to order Uriah into the front lines placed himself in Joab's power. David had reacted with great indignation when Joab had assassinated his rival Abner; now he was asking Joab to do a similar deed for himself: 'Put Uriah in the front line, where the fighting is heaviest, then retreat and let him be killed' (2 Sam. 11:15). As Joab pocketed that letter with an ironic smile, he must have known that he would never hear about Abner again. He now knew some things about David that David would never want to be made public. The balance of power shifted subtly. David had made himself hostage to his subordinate. There was not only a criminal as prime minister, the King himself was compromised.

WHAT TO DO WITH SIN

- *Admit it!* Not until Nathan cleared away the fog from David's rationalizing mind did David recognize his conduct for what it was, give it its name and admit it as sin: 'I have sinned against the LORD' (2 Sam. 12:13), David said simply to Nathan.

In Psalm 51, written afterwards, he plumbed the depths of agonizing penitence: 'I recognize my faults; I am always conscious of my sins. I have sinned against you – only against you – and done what you consider evil' (Ps. 51:3-4).

- *Accept the consequences!* 'So you are right in judging me; you are justified in condemning me. I have been evil from the day I was born; from the time I was conceived, I have been sinful' (vv. 4-5). As at Ziklag David again showed his willingness to accept the consequences of his actions. When Nathan prophesied that the child born to Bathsheba would die, David fasted and prayed to God to spare the child's life. But when the child did die, David washed himself, worshipped in God's house and returned to the palace to eat. To his officials, who were mystified by his behaviour, David explained, 'I did fast and weep while he was still alive. I thought that the LORD might be merciful to me and not let the child die. But now that he is dead, why should I fast? Could I bring the child back to life? I will some day go to where he is, but he can never come back to me' (2 Sam. 12:22-23). Probably the main mark of genuine repentance is the willingness to accept the consequences of our sin.

- *Ask for forgiveness!* 'Wash away all my evil and make me clean from my sin!…Remove my sin, and I will be clean; wash me, and I will be whiter than snow' (Ps. 51:2, 7).

- *Ask for the power to live differently.* 'Create a pure heart in me, O God, and put a new and loyal spirit in me. Do not banish me from your presence; do not take your holy spirit away from me. Give me again the joy that comes from your salvation, and make me willing to obey you' (Ps. 51:10-12).

TWO CONSEQUENCES

In time David arose to live again by the mercy of God. 'Then David comforted his wife Bathsheba. He had intercourse with her, and she bore a son, whom David named Solomon. The LORD loved the boy and commanded the prophet Nathan to name the boy Jedidiah, because the LORD loved him' (2 Sam. 12:24-25). The story of David and Bathsheba had two consequences. One is positive. Solomon was blessed by God with wisdom and he was successor to David's throne. In the very relationship with Bathsheba, where David had sinned, and in response to his penitence, the mercy of God was shown.

There were very negative consequences also. Nathan pronounced them in advance.

- *Hereditary Violence.* Nathan's message from the LORD was, 'Now, in every generation some of your descendants will die a violent death because you have disobeyed me and have taken Uriah's wife' (12:10). The rest of the historical books of the Bible are evidence that this actually happened.

- *Family Feuds.* The LORD said, 'I swear to you that I will cause someone from your own family to bring trouble on you' (12:11). Family feuds plagued the rest of David's life, especially in the sons, who were far from knowing David's God. This was notoriously seen in the rebellion of Absalom. David himself saw the end of his long history of poorly controlled passion in the way his family turned out.

- *Public Humiliation.* The LORD said, 'You will see it when I take your wives from you and give them to another man; and he will have intercourse with them in broad daylight. You sinned in secret, but I will make this happen in broad daylight for all Israel to see' (12:11-12). Absalom was the one who made this a reality (16:21-22). David discovered that the effects of sin in his private life would spill over into his public life, and he could not contain the damage.

It is wonderfully true that God forgives sin and we know this especially since the death of Jesus on the cross. But the consequences of sin remain and we will have no choice but to face them.

Private and Public Morality

The question is often asked as to whether sexual infidelity disqualifies a person from public leadership. David continued as king. Nathan did not depose him. Whether he was better or worse after this we need to judge from the story.

At the personal level, the answer has to be that sexual passion can cloud the judgment and often does. That seems incontrovertible. It is also a biblical position that infidelity in marriage threatens the factor of faithfulness in all the rest of a person's relationships. I see this in the very frequent analogy that is drawn by the prophets between adultery and the people's forsaking of their God. It is almost as though God has made the test and touchstone of human faithfulness the marriage relationship.

In society, however, the consequences of David's sin are seen for years, indeed for generations to come. No man is an island. All that we do has consequences. We live in a moral universe and we weaken that moral fabric every time we sin. A family, a city, a nation may not see the consequences of the sins of its leaders immediately. They will reap what the people and their leaders have sown over the years and generations.

There is an interesting twist in the story affecting Joab who had carried out David's orders. 'Meanwhile Joab continued his campaign against Rabbah... He sent messengers to David to report: "I have attacked Rabbah and have captured its water supply. Now gather the rest of your forces, attack the city and take it yourself. I don't want to get the credit for capturing it."' It looks as though even Joab had not been best pleased with his king's conduct.

But there was mercy. The world has a very limited understanding of this story. David's eighth wife appears on the first page of the New

Testament as one of the forebears of Jesus the Messiah and Saviour of the world. She is not called Bathsheba. The stain is still there. She is still described as the person who had been the wife of Uriah. But she is caught up in the noblest genealogy of all.

It is not our mistakes but what we do with them that determines the kind of person we become. '[I]f we confess our sins to God, he will keep his promise and do what is right: he will forgive us our sins and purify us from all our wrongdoing' (1 John 1:9).

Today's Challenges:

How to handle depression.
A leader and his own children.

'For if a man does not know how to manage his own family,
how can he take care of the church of God?'
(1 Tim. 3:5)

22
Life in the Palace

2 Samuel 5:13-16; 9:1-13; 13–14

THE HEIGHT OF GENEROSITY

The recorded life of the palace started with a person moving in whom no one expected to be there. He was a cripple in both legs, disabled from a fall when he was a child. What is more, he was the grandson of King Saul, David's greatest enemy. But he was also the son of Jonathan, who had been David's greatest friend.

When David was settling in to the comparative luxury of his new palace, he remembered Jonathan and asked if there were any survivors from Saul's family whom he could honour for Jonathan's sake. Ziba, one of Saul's servants, told him about Mephibosheth who was actually Jonathan's own son. David, with extreme generosity, restored to Mephibosheth all the lands that had belonged to his grandfather and appointed Ziba to manage them. He brought Mephibosheth to live at the palace and he ate at the king's table, just like one of the king's sons. He would have been older than the eldest son of the king by five or more years. It was a magnanimous act.

DARK DAYS AHEAD

Bathsheba came to live in the palace. This began more than a decade of dark days in the royal household. The chronology of David's reign is impossible to reconstruct with any accuracy. If, however, we take all the references to time in the story, we can make approximate guestimates about the relative ages of the people involved. David would have been about fifty when he brought Bathsheba to the palace. He obviously loved her and her son Solomon, but the palace began to go through a series of dysfunctional relationships that bore out the prophecies that Nathan had made after the Bathsheba incident (2 Sam. 12:10-12).

It began with Amnon, David's first-born, when he was around twenty years of age. He fell hopelessly in love with his stepsister Tamar, probably in her mid-to-late teens but kept quite secluded from the rest of her many brothers and their children. With the help of a cousin, Amnon got her into his house. When he sought to have consenting sex with her, she tried to dissuade him by raising the question of the shame it would bring on him and on her. 'Such a thing should not be done in Israel... You would be like one of the wicked fools in Israel' (2 Sam. 13:12, 13NIV). How hollow it must have sounded to both of them. She was trying to bolt the stable door after the horse had gone. He could have responded that it was in fact kingly to do what he was proposing after their father's behaviour with Bathsheba. He did not. He raped her and saw his love turn immediately to hate and threw her out of his house.

She was a full sister of Absalom, David's third son, and of royal blood on their mother's side. Tamar wandered around distraught and humiliated and was rescued by her brother Absalom and taken into his house for refuge. He urged her not to say anything. After all, Amnon was presumed to be heir to the throne. David heard about the rape and was furious, but did nothing about it. What could he say with the memory still fresh of how he himself had behaved with Bathsheba?

THE FIRST SILENCE

Absalom took no immediate action but was filled with hate for Amnon and refused to speak to him for two years. All this time he was planning revenge. This was difficult when the king himself was doing nothing about it. There had been no endorsement of the principle of primogeniture that the eldest son would succeed to the throne. This had not been part of the promise made to David by God through Nathan, the prophet, when he was assured his descendants would sit on his throne. This must have caused great uncertainty and rivalry between the royal princes.

At the end of two years Absalom invited all the royal family except the King to elaborate sheepshearing festivities some miles north of Jerusalem. There with all his stepbrothers present he got Amnon drunk and had him killed. David mourned a long time for Amnon, but again took no action. He must have been reminded of his own behaviour towards Uriah, Bathsheba's husband, whom he had made drunk and then later had killed.

THREE YEARS OF EXILE

Amnon's death left Absalom as the oldest living son of David. It is generally assumed that Chileab, the second son had died. Fearing the wrath of the king, he went into exile at the court of his mother's people about 100 miles to the north. When David's sorrow for Amnon had abated, he began to long to see Absalom who was a very attractive young man. He could not, it would seem, bring himself to do anything about recalling him. Inertia seemed to have taken David over.

PARABLE NUMBER TWO

Joab, David's commander-in-chief, sensed how the king was really feeling and devised a scheme to persuade him to recall Absalom. He found an unknown, but very resourceful, woman from the hill country of Judah. He rehearsed her in a sob story designed to open the king's mind to bringing Absalom back to Jerusalem. It hinged on a classic case of the lesser of two evils. She pretended to be a widow, one of whose sons had killed the other, his only brother. Relatives were demanding that the remaining son be executed for murder, leaving her without any son and her former husband without heir. She acted the part well and David was persuaded to recall Absalom. David detected Joab's hand behind the woman's story and ordered him to travel north to bring Absalom back after three years away.

THE SECOND SILENCE

Absalom was back in Jerusalem but not in the palace. He was in his own house. The king still refused to see or speak to him for another two years. It is not difficult to imagine the tense and gloomy atmosphere that must have pervaded the palace, first with Absalom not speaking to Amnon for two years and then David not speaking to Absalom for two years after three years of exile. Absalom felt he was no better off than he had been in exile. Eventually, he managed to enlist Joab's help again to break the deadlock. Again Joab succeeded and David welcomed him to the palace. A kiss ended five long years of total rejection by his father.

This is a very different David from the person we have watched in earlier life. All his initiative seems to have drained away. He seems to be suffering from the paralysing effect of guilt. Not surprisingly, his attention to the affairs of state suffered. People came up from the country with suits and petitions to present, and there was no one appointed to hear their cases. David's popularity in the country, that had been so high, began to wane. This consequence of David's adultery and murder of Uriah is not so well known or recognized as the deed itself.

It resulted in a dysfunctional royal family. Part of it was no doubt due to his failure to discipline his children (1 Kings 1:6). Part of it was no doubt due to his aping of the kings of other nations. He found himself coping with a polygamous family.

POLYGAMY

The Bible with regard to polygamy is ambiguous. To say that the Old Testament allows polygamy is to speak only half the truth. Adam, Cain, Noah and his three sons, all seem to have had only one wife. This is the beginning to which Jesus refers when he speaks to the Pharisees about divorce, saying, 'It was not like that at the time of creation' (Matt. 19:8). In the beginning monogamy, or one man married to one wife for life, was the ideal. In the less godly line described in Genesis, six generations removed from Cain, Lamech started the process by taking two wives. He is the first polygamist mentioned in Scripture.

Although the Law of Moses discourages rather than bans having more than one wife, the Old Testament gives no picture of contented polygamy. Invariably the story throbs with pain and unhappiness. Abraham had several wives whose unhappy story ended with tragic consequences, still multiplied to this day in the hatred between Jew and Arab. Jacob had several wives, breeding disunity and trouble in his home and in his descendants. Elkanah had two wives, who filled his home with bitter rivalry (1 Sam. 1:1-8). Jesus emphasizes that a plurality of wives, even serially by divorce, was not God's intention for mankind: 'It was not like that at the creation' (Matt. 19:8). David's case is one of the unhappiest. He seems not to have known what he wanted or what he needed in a wife, and had little opportunity to learn. He moved his attentions from one wife to another, multiplying his harem. Although he knew that he would become king, he married three wives before his coronation. After his succession to the throne he added five wives, plus several concubines. David's failure in this part of the Law produced a family story of pain and tragedy. 'What boots it at one gate to make defense,' wrote Milton in *Samson Agonistes*, 'and at another to let in the foe?'

THE TIDE RUNS OUT

Absalom, once he was reinstated to the capital, lost no time in capitalising on the disfavour into which the king was slipping. He was a very handsome man, perhaps a second generation version of what David had been in his twenties. He set out to court the popularity that the king was losing.

He 'provided a chariot and horses for himself, and an escort of fifty men. He would get up early and go and stand by the road at the city gate. Whenever someone came there with a dispute that he wanted the king to settle, Absalom would call him over and ask him where he was from. And after the man had told him what tribe he was from, Absalom would say, "Look, the law is on your side, but there is no representative of the king to hear your case." And he would add, 'How I wish I were a judge! Then anyone who had a dispute or a claim could come to me, and I would give him justice. "When the man approached Absalom to bow down before him, Absalom would reach out, take hold of him, and kiss him. Absalom did this with every Israelite who came to the king for justice, and so he won their loyalty."

MORALITY

The only person who brings God into the conversation in this portrait of David's family in action, or inaction, is the wise widow whom Joab hired to talk to David. 'She said, "Your Majesty, please pray to the LORD your God, so that my relative who is responsible for avenging the death of my son will not commit a greater crime by killing my other son." "I promise by the living LORD," David replied, "that your son will not be harmed in the least." Later she observed, 'your promise, sir, would make me safe, because the king is like God's angel and can distinguish good from evil. May the LORD your God be with you!' Ironically, David took her advice about recalling Joab, but ignored her way of bringing God into the situation. The result was the days of gloom that we have described.

TODAY'S CHALLENGES:

Stick to first principles.
Overcome evil with good.

'Christ... left you an example,
so that you would follow in his steps...
when he suffered, he did not threaten,
but placed his hopes in God, the righteous Judge.'
(1 Peter 2:21-23)

23

To Live Again

2 Samuel 14–17; Psalms 3; 55

AN UNSURPRISING COUP

David was now in his early sixties. The graph of his effectiveness as a king and as a person had been at a low level for more than a decade since the shady acquisition of Bathsheba, his eighth wife. The dominant figure in national life was now his son and possible heir, Absalom, who was in his early thirties. He was putting himself forward with a great show of pomp and flair, and putting his father down by insinuating that he was an aging and somewhat incompetent ruler.

After four years of self-promotion, Absalom made his move. Under cover of fulfilling a vow, made earlier, to worship the LORD in Hebron, he went there, about twenty miles away. He took a retinue of 200 men who knew nothing of what he had in mind, Clandestinely, however, he sent couriers to all the tribes of Israel to inform them that he was becoming king in Hebron and invite their support. The positive response was encouraging to him and alarming to the king when he heard of it.

Hebron was in Judah and was the place where David had been first crowned king of Judah thirty years previously. There seems to be something of a tribal bias to this coup. This is reinforced by Absalom recalling from retirement, in a nearby town in Judah a trusted counsellor of David called Ahitophel.

NO COLLATERAL DAMAGE

From what we know of David's behaviour in the past decade we are not surprised that he took the line of least resistance to this first attempted coup. He ordered the evacuation of his men from Jerusalem. He did not want his precious city to be destroyed or its new citizens killed. It became clear that, however this evacuation began, it developed not into a rout, but into a strategic retreat. Something of the old David began to revive. His strategic sense was activated by events, and he began to behave with something of his own distinctive flair, born of his own earlier, distinctive values.

There are two possible reasons for this gradual recovery. One was the discovery of the number and quality of those who remained loyal to him and showed it. In fact, it was a great tribute to the person he had been that so many were still ready to stand by him to the death. The other reason was that he began to view the whole event as a test of where he stood with God after his poor record. More worked for him than against him, and hope revived.

MERCENARIES BECOME DEVOTED FOLLOWERS

As he came to the city boundary, he offered to free his personal bodyguard, the 600 mercenaries led by Ittai the Gittite. 'Why are you going with us? Go back and stay with the new king. You are a foreigner, a refugee away from your own country. You have lived here only a short time, so why should I make you wander round with me? I don't even know where I'm going. Go back and take your fellow-countrymen with you and may the LORD be kind and faithful to you' (2 Sam. 15:19-20).

David was giving his mercenaries a chance to disentangle themselves from this dispute in his own family. He was willing to let his hired troops go rather than involve them in the consequences of his own misdeeds. The allegiance of Ittai's soldiers had been bought with money, but they stayed out of respect and devotion: 'I swear to you in the LORD's name that I will always go with you wherever you go, even if it means death,' said Ittai (2 Sam. 15:21).

HE REFUSED TO TRY AND MANIPULATE GOD

As David's followers left Jerusalem, Zadok the priest stood at the gate with the Levites carrying the Ark of the Covenant, the symbol of God's presence. David had brought the Ark into the city with great ceremony and enthusiasm, making Jerusalem the holy city. He had brought God into the civic affairs of his capital. Now that David was leaving, the priests decided that he had a right to take the Ark with him. David, however, remembered the battle of Shiloh, where the Israelites had tried to manipulate God by carrying the Ark of the Covenant into battle against the Philistines. Instead of bringing victory, the Ark had been captured and the Israelites defeated. The nation learned then that they could not, with the physical symbol, manipulate God. Instead they had to correct what displeased God.

David's experience taught him that he had forfeited any claim on God, and he refused to try to use the Almighty for his own purposes. He told Zadok, and his two sons, 'Take the Covenant Box back to the city. If the LORD is pleased with me, some day he will let me come back to see it and the place where it stays. But if he isn't pleased with me well, then, let him do to me what he wishes' (2 Sam. 15:25-26). Like Jesus, his greater son, who faced his death and refused to call down legions of angels to deliver him. David did not try to use God.

A STRATEGIC PRAYER

When he heard that Ahithophel had joined Absalom's revolution, he prayed: 'Please, LORD, turn Ahithophel's advice into nonsense!'

(2 Sam.15:31). Ahithophel and David had been lifelong friends and companions. David so respected Ahithophel's judgment that he made him his principal adviser. He did nothing without consulting him, and repeatedly the wisdom and judgment of this man forwarded the interests of David's throne. But Ahithophel had a granddaughter named Bathsheba, and after David's adultery with her Ahithophel turned on David, left the court and returned to his ancestral town of Giloh. When Absalom organized his revolution, he made a bid for the political skill of Ahithophel, confident that his bitterness and disillusionment with David would bring him into the conspiracy. When the news reached David that Ahithophel had gone with Absalom, he could only turn to prayer and hope that God in his mercy would protect him from the skill and wisdom of this man whose granddaughter he had violated.

He elaborated on how he felt in Psalm 55. 'Confuse the speech of my enemies, O LORD! I see violence and riots in the city, surrounding it day and night, filling it with crime and trouble. There is destruction everywhere; the streets are full of oppression and fraud. If it were an enemy that mocked me, I could endure it; if it were an opponent boasting over me, I could hide myself from him. But it is you, my companion, my colleague and close friend. We had intimate talks with each other and worshipped together in the Temple.'

AN INTELLIGENCE NETWORK

David's other adviser, Hushai, remained faithful to the King. He sent him back to Jerusalem to Absalom, hoping that God would use Hushai's loyalty to counter Ahithophel's bitterness. With his two prime political advisers in the rebel court of his son, David left the outcome to God, either chastisement through Ahithophel or mercy through Hushai. With the acumen of a seasoned soldier, however, he arranged for Ahimahaz and Jonathan, the two sons of Zadok the priest, to be ready to be couriers to bring him intelligence as to what advice Absalom was being given.

David wrote this Psalm as he ran from Absalom: 'I have so many enemies, LORD, so many who turn against me! They talk about me and say, "God will not help him." But you, O LORD, are always my shield from danger; you give me victory and restore my courage. I call to the LORD for help, and from his sacred hill he answers me. I lie down and sleep, and all night long the LORD protects me. I am not afraid of the thousands of enemies who surround me on every side. Come, LORD! Save me, my God! You punish all my enemies and leave them powerless to harm me. Victory comes from the LORD may he bless his people' (Ps. 3).

In the event, Ahithophel's advice, which turned out to be sound, was ignored and Hushai's followed, greatly to David's advantage. The historian underlines how much David's prayer was answered. 'The LORD had decided that Ahithophel's good advice would not be followed, so that disaster would come on Absalom' (2 Sam. 17:14). One can only imagine how Bathsheba felt when the news came about her grandfather, 'When Ahithophel saw that his advice had not been followed, he saddled his donkey and went back to his own city. After putting his affairs in order, he hanged himself. He was buried in the family grave.'

Tribal Factors

Two incidents reminded David that there were others from his past that he might have to fear. The first was Ziba, the servant of Mephibosheth, Jonathan's son, whom David had brought to eat at his table. He arrived with a train of animals loaded with provisions for David and his army. When asked, he alleged that Mephibosheth had elected to throw in his lot with Absalom, hoping that the kingdom of his grandfather Saul might be restored to him. David accepted his unsubstantiated word and transferred Mephibosheth's lands to Ziba, perhaps as a signal that it would pay the people from Benjamin to stay on the side of the king.

The second incident was more vicious. As David was leaving Jerusalem he met a relative of Saul named Shimei. He had nursed bitterness and resentment against David through all the years of his reign and now pelted David's troops with clods and curses: 'Get out! Get out! Murderer! Criminal! You took Saul's kingdom, and now the LORD is punishing you for murdering so many of Saul's family. The LORD has given the kingdom to your son Absalom, and you are ruined, you murderer!' (2 Sam. 16:7-8).

Abishai, Joab's brother, asked whether he should go over and take Shimei's head off. David refused. He knew that Shimei's accusations were untrue. He had scrupulously treated Saul and all his family with honour and respect. In other respects, however, he knew his sins to be worse than anyone could describe. Whatever people chose to believe or to say behind his back made little difference:

"If he curses me because the LORD told him to, who has the right to ask why he does it?"... "My own son is trying to kill me; so why should you be surprised at this Benjaminite? The LORD told him to curse; so leave him alone and let him do it. Perhaps the LORD will notice my misery and give me some blessings to take the place of his curse" (2 Sam. 16:10-12). David had the protection of a broken and contrite heart, which gave him security in God.

THE BATTLE

Absalom entered Jerusalem, stole his father's concubines, amassed an army and marched out to fight against the old King's loyal forces. As they moved into battle positions, David gave explicit instructions to his captains, for his sake, to deal gently with Absalom. He was not vindictive. He did not call down the wrath of God on his rebel son. He knew only grief to see him ranged against him.

In his younger days David had been tempted to be vindictive. He had set out in anger to destroy Nabal and all his household over a small matter of a few roasted sheep. Abigail had saved him from that, and he had learned his lesson well. Now he was relearning that principle.

He did not rejoice in the unsought death of Absalom but seemed to hope to the end that he would change. In the face of possible disaster, David's character showed through. All his previous experiences came to his aid, and he displayed that meekness that Jesus said inherits the earth.

How David Handled Victory (2 Sam. 18–19)

Success is a greater test of a person than failure. What a man does when he is down, when he faces defeat, displays the kind of man he is. An even greater test of character is what a man does when he is up, in the flush of victory. In Absalom's revolution David faced both tests. He was ousted from the capital in the *coup d'etat* led by his son. He regrouped his men under the officers who remained loyal and eventually defeated Absalom's army in the forests of Ephraim. David then faced the more severe test. Could he suffer without bitterness?

Loving Enemies

It began even before the battle. Absalom, the rebel, was to be spared (2 Sam.18:5). Afterwards messengers ran to David with news of the battle. His only question was, 'Is the young man Absalom safe?' (2 Sam.18:29, 32). When the battle had been won and Absalom killed by Joab, David felt only grief: 'O my son! My son Absalom! Absalom, my son! If only I had died in your place, my son! Absalom, my son!' (2 Sam. 18:33). Unable to understand how an enemy could be loved, Joab complained about David's sorrow: 'You oppose those who love you and support those who hate you! 'You have made it clear that your officers and men mean nothing to you. I can see that you would be quite happy if Absalom were alive today and all of us were dead' (2 Sam. 19:6). His complaint was exaggerated, but he accurately gauged the extent to which David had wanted reconciliation. He never ceased to love his enemy, and the token was the fact that he dismissed Joab from his post and found a new commander-in-chief (2 Sam. 19:13).

DOING GOOD TO THOSE WHO HATE YOU

The Israelites who had backed Absalom fled to their homes after the battle. David again moved to overcome evil with good. He did not rush back to Jerusalem or seek revenge on the leaders of the rebellion. Instead he fell back on his principle of rule by the consent of the people. He had followed this when he became king (2 Sam. 1–5). When he heard that people throughout the country were saying, 'why doesn't somebody try to bring King David back?' (2 Sam. 19:10), he sent a message to the tribe of Judah, to the very centre of the rebellion in Hebron: 'Why should you be the last to help bring the king back to his palace? You are my relatives, my own flesh and blood' (2 Sam. 19:11-12). Instead of confrontation, David offered them a chance to redeem themselves; instead of reprisals, he offered friendship. He still called them brothers. He promoted Amasa, who had commanded Absalom's army: 'You are my relative. From now on I am putting you in charge of the army in place of Joab' (2 Sam. 19:13).

When the northern tribes and the tribe of Judah started quarrelling over who had remained more loyal to David (2 Sam. 19:40-43), and when a Benjaminite named Sheba led another abortive rebellion against David (2 Sam. 20:1-22) based on the old tribal rivalry between Judah and Benjamin, David wanted only the restoration of order with the minimum loss of life.

THE WAY BACK

On his way back to Jerusalem, David's old friend Shimei arrived, bringing with him a thousand men from the tribe of Benjamin. No longer cursing the King, he fell on his face in front of David. 'Your Majesty, please forget the wrong I did that day you left Jerusalem.

Don't hold it against me or think about it any more. I know, sir, that I have sinned, and this is why I am the first one from the northern tribes to come and meet Your Majesty today' (2 Sam. 19:19-20). Abishai urged execution, but again David chose magnanimity. He rebuked Abishai and forgave Shimei (2 Sam. 19:23). People who have a true view of themselves before God cannot be hurt by what others say of them. He maintained his equanimity with Ziba when Mephibosheth told him he had not defected to Absalom.

Such were the approaches David used to consolidate his restoration to the throne. He pursued the way of peace. Political madness? Impractical ethics for public life? Perhaps. But in his handling of this tragic rebellion, David simply anticipated the way of his even greater descendant who taught, 'Love your enemies, do good to those who hate you, bless those who curse you' (Luke 6:27). Jesus added, 'pray for those who ill-treat you.' There are no such prayers in this part of 2 Samuel, but there are in the Psalms of David. There he struggled in the presence of God with his vindictiveness and showed how great a fight it was to behave as he did in this instance and how much prayer was essential in the process.

In the life of David we are dealing with something much greater than the behaviour of one ancient ruler. He was the first real king of Israel. He was breaking new ground around 1000 BC. He provides a backdrop for the rest of the Old Testament. He was forming the concept of what we now know as the Kingdom of God. It did not come to fruition in the kingdom of Israel. This kingdom had to split and then disappear. But the concepts were retained and developed by psalmists and prophets, like Isaiah. Eventually the Kingdom of God was initiated by Jesus, great David's greater son. We are privileged to be part of it today. The challenge is whether we will live according to its principles or according to the fashion of this world.

TODAY'S CHALLENGES:

Damage limitation.
The right and wrong appeal to numbers.

Paul said, 'the Lord rescued me from them all'.
(2 Tim. 3:11)

24
Aftershocks from Absalom's Earthquake

2 Samuel 19–24

TRIBAL TROUBLE

For more than thirty years in David's story all we hear about is Israel and all Israel. There is very little about Judah or the other tribes, and nothing to indicate tension between the tribes. Even in the Psalms six tribes are never mentioned. Three are mentioned only once. The remainder are in single digits. This was David's great achievement. It was helped that he located himself and his headquarters in Jerusalem, which was technically outside any tribal area.

That solidarity began to be undermined when Absalom made his bid to oust his father and become king himself. He started his insurrection in Hebron, a notable city in Judah. Yet, at the same time he sent messages to all Israel about his intentions and called on them to acknowledge him. The story of the battle with David reads as though Absalom's army was principally from all Israel. His call for support had been heeded.

This line-up made things complicated when Absalom, their new king, was killed in battle. What were his followers to do? Who else was there to follow now? And how would David treat those who had defected to Absalom? There was a big vacuum.

His Israelite supporters followed the usual pattern and slunk off home hoping they could disappear into the normal life of their communities. There were, however, lots of discussions as to the best way they should handle the situation. Some began to talk of returning to David's side and getting him back to Jerusalem and the throne (2 Sam. 19:9-14).

Word of this debate reached David, who was still east of the Jordan River, and he decided to take some action. He sent two priests to ask the elders of Judah why they were being so slow in moving to bring him back to Jerusalem. He appealed to the fact that they were his own relatives. He even made the conciliatory move to appoint his nephew Amasa to replace Joab in charge of the army. Joab had killed Absalom in defiance of the King's orders. Amasa had been Absalom's general. The appointment was popular and helped to win back the loyalty of all the men of Judah.

So now there were two competing reception parties when he crossed back over the Jordan to Gilgal: all the people of Judah and half the people of Israel. The people of Israel accused those from Judah of trying to monopolise the King. The people of Judah argued that the king was one of them. The Israelites retorted that they had ten times as many claims on King David, as they had ten tribes to their one. It was quite a dispute and the men of Judah were more violent in making their claims than the men of Israel.

A NEW REBEL LEADER

Into the middle of this fracas stepped a worthless character called Sheba, from Benjamin. He sounded a trumpet and began to chant, 'Down with David! We won't follow him! Men of Israel, let's go home!' He got a ready ear and the Israelites began to desert and followed Sheba to the north. The men of Judah remained loyal and escorted David back up to Jerusalem. Civil war seemed imminent.

BACK IN THE CITY

First David let the men of Judah go home while he settled his own domestic arrangements. But David was now back in active mode, more like his old self. He called Amasa, his new commander-in-chief, and ordered him to mobilize the troops from Judah again and be back with them in the city in two days. Amasa set out but failed to get back in the specified time. David saw the danger as really serious so he told his other nephew, Abishai, to take the mercenaries and go after Sheba and prevent him from consolidating his position. They mounted up and left, ostensibly with Joab serving under his brother, Abishai.

They encountered Amasa and his muster at Gibeon, about ten miles north. Joab went to greet Amasa, who was his cousin, letting his sword fall out as he did so. Grabbing Amasa with one hand by the beard to kiss him, and picking up the sword in the other hand, he deftly stabbed and killed the man David had tried to put in his place as Commander-in-Chief.

It was awkward with Amasa's body lying bleeding in the road. Joab and Abishai did not hesitate. They rode off in pursuit of Sheba. One of Joab's men had the wit to call out, 'Everyone who is for Joab and David, follow Joab!' Another dragged the body off the road and covered it with a blanket in a field. Then the two troops fell in behind their commanders and resumed their search for Sheba.

DEATH IN THE CITY

It was a long march. Sheba and his small band of relatives did not stop until they had gone north about 100 miles and took refuge in a remote city called Abel. The pursuing army settled down for a lengthy siege. After some days a wise woman called to Joab. She loved her city and did not want it or her people destroyed. She assured Joab that Abel was one of the most peaceful and loyal cities in Israel; Joab said they had no quarrel with the city or its people. He asked for her to arrange for Sheba to be handed over and they would withdraw. She persuaded her people and they cut off Sheba's head and threw it over the wall. The army returned home to Jerusalem and the King, without any further explanation than that. The first aftershock had been survived.

UNFINISHED BUSINESS

A three-year famine forced David to pray to the LORD to find out if there were any possible explanations for it. It turned out that, somewhere along the line, perhaps in his early over-enthusiastic days, Saul had tried to rectify a centuries-old anomaly. When Joshua occupied the land of Canaan, one enterprising community in a town called Gibeon performed one of the classic cases of deception in history. It was successful and they got a treaty that allowed them to stay on in their town and not be destroyed. The only penalty was that they would be 'hewers of wood and drawers of water' in perpetuity. Saul, apparently decided that this had to end and in contravention of their treaty had many of them killed. David got the word from the LORD that this was why the famine had been sent. He asked the people of Gibeon what he could do to make up for the wrong that had been done to them. They requested that a token seven male descendants of Saul should be ritually hanged in what had been Saul's town.

This was a problem for David who had studiously avoided anything that could be construed as revenge on Saul. Nonetheless, in the circumstances, David complied with this extreme request. It led to a remarkable show of devotion to the dead on the part of Rispah, Saul's granddaughter. This moved David further to see to it that Saul and all his family were given proper burial in the family tomb. After that God answered their prayers for the country. The second aftershock had been survived.

A DEADLY CENSUS

David seemed to be on a roll in his regained activism to restore the unity Absalom had undermined. This did not altogether please God, and he let David go a step too far. It was a logical step, but a step too far. He let him organize the first census in the nation of Israel.

You have to go back to the time in the wilderness to find the last time the people had been counted. There was one count at the beginning and one at the end of the trek through Sinai (Num.1 & 26). Right from the beginning there was a wariness about any census. They had to make a special offering for everyone counted, 'so that no disaster will come on him while the census is being taken' (Exod. 30:11-12). There is often a serious dislike of censuses because they are usually the prelude to taxation, conscription to the army, or recruitment for forced labour.

Oddly enough, Joab, not a particularly religious man, was the one who did his best to dissuade David from counting the people. David was adamant and with great efficiency the enumerators traveled the length and breadth of the country. They ascertained the number of those capable of military service, 800,000 in Israel and 500,000 in Judah. Now he knew where he stood statistically, he could plan accordingly. It is a strange story. No sooner did he have the numbers than he began to have serious doubts about what he had done. In a way that we are learning to expect of David, he came to the LORD in great distress, 'I have committed a terrible sin in doing this! Please forgive me. I have acted foolishly.'

This time a new prophet, Gad, was sent to give him three choices. 'Three years of famine in your land or three months of running away from your enemies or three days of an epidemic in your land? David's answer was characteristic of him. "Let the LORD himself be the one to punish us, for he is merciful." So the LORD sent an epidemic on Israel. Seventy thousand Israelites died. 'When the LORD's angel was about to destroy Jerusalem, the LORD changed his mind about punishing the people and said to the angel who was killing them, "Stop! That's enough!" The angel was by the threshing place of Araunah, a Jebusite.

'David saw the angel who was killing the people, and said to the Lord, "I am the guilty one. I am the one who did wrong. What have these poor people done? You should punish me and my family."'

A Sacred Spot

Simultaneously, Gad instructed David, 'Go up to Araunah's threshing-place and build an altar to the Lord.' David went. Araunah looked down and saw the king and his officials coming up to him. He threw himself on the ground in front of David and asked, 'Your Majesty, why are you here?'

David answered, "To buy your threshing place and build an altar for the Lord, in order to stop the epidemic." "Take it, Your Majesty," Araunah said, "and offer to the Lord whatever you wish. Here are these oxen to burn as an offering on the altar; here are their yokes and the threshing boards to use as fuel." Araunah gave it all to the king and said to him, "May the Lord your God accept your offering."

But the king answered, "No, I will pay you for it. I will not offer to the Lord my God sacrifices that have cost me nothing." And he bought the threshing-place and the oxen for fifty pieces of silver. Then he built an altar to the Lord and offered burnt-offerings and fellowship-offerings. The Lord answered his prayer, and the epidemic in Israel was stopped.' The third aftershock had been survived at not a little cost.

This spot became one of the most important in history. On it were built the temples under Solomon, Zerubbabel and Herod. Today it is within the Dome of the Rock in Jerusalem. Such are the ways of God.

TODAY'S CHALLENGE:

Take care whom you appoint.

> Paul said, 'Take the teachings that you heard me
> proclaim in the presence of many witnesses, and entrust them
> to reliable people, who will be able to teach others also.'
> (2 Tim. 2:2)

25
The Politics of Leadership

2 Samuel passim; 1 Kings 2:28-35

DEFAULT NEPOTISM

Joab, David's general, is probably the person who plays the most important role in the king's life, at least from the time he became king. He was David's nephew, although they were probably similar in age. He was the son of David's stepsister Zeruiah and they may have grown up together in the extended family of Jesse in Bethlehem.

Nepotes is the Latin for nephews. Nephews is what the illegitimate children of corrupt popes were called. These were favoured and promoted in papal appointments in church and state. This practice came to be called nepotism, the form of corruption that promotes relatives to positions for which they may not be well fitted. David's appointing Joab is an ancient example of this practice. David appointed a nephew as his Number Two. He kept power in the family.

Default is a word used with computers to indicate any program or setting that will be used unless different instructions are given. To use it with nepotism is to recognize that it is very natural and normal to favour relatives. There is nothing necessarily wrong in promoting relatives if they are the best person for the job.

The question we must ask is, 'Was Joab the best person to be Number Two to David, and how did his behaviour contribute or detract from David's reign?' There is no doubt that Joab was a very able person militarily, very courageous, bold and ambitious, a Mr Fixit. Fortunately we can approach the question from statements that David himself made.

A CRIME OVERLOOKED

See Chapter 15

There was a good chance that David might have had Abner, Saul's commander, as his second-in-command. Abner was in the process of securing the support of all the northern tribes for David. He was authorized by David to do this. Before he could even go about consolidating the work he had already done to enlist them, Joab killed him in cold blood in revenge for the death of his brother Asahel, which Asahel had brought on himself. Joab murdered him even although he had been guaranteed a safe passage by David. In doing this, Joab jeopardised a very sensitive and essential political process in mid-course. He also prevented David from getting a more experienced general from the ranks of the other tribes to help him rule the newly united country.

All his life David saw this as a heinous crime. He said so before he died (1 Kings 2:5-6). Yet he failed to deal with Joab at the time. The most he was willing to do was to put on a great funeral for Abner at which he spoke the eulogy and uttered a powerful curse upon Joab. It was only words! He left the murdered alone. He was his nephew. He put a criminal in charge.

I AM WEAK TODAY

This is what David said at the time, and he was weak. He was only king in Judah. He was years away from being accepted as king of all Israel, and there was no guarantee that this would happen. It was interesting what he said next. '[T]he sons of Zeruiah are too hard for me'(ASV). They were too ruthless, too violent. David saw that this also made him weak. He had constantly to rescue his reputation from the slurs cast upon it by his nephew, Joab. Joab took the actions. David was left with the blame, for he was his nephew.

COLLUSION

See Chapter 17

It was not all one-sided. When David threw out the challenge, 'Does anybody here hate the Jebusites as much as I do? Enough to kill them?' 'The first man to kill a Jebusite will be commander of the army', it is hard to believe that he did not say to himself, 'It will be Joab! He will not let it be anyone else.' In the event, Joab was the first to get into the city and to become David's Number Two by default, really. It was not a deliberate appointment taken in the light of Joab's character and experience. He already knew Joab well, too well. Yet he made the appointment by a lottery which Joab took care to win. No doubt David salved his conscience about it by pretending that the test had some validity and it could be looked on as a providential intervention (2 Sam. 5:6-8; 1 Chron. 11:4-9). He let the criminal stay.

See Chapter 21

Clearly Joab reciprocated this mutual collaboration. When David needed Bathsheba's husband, Uriah, disposed of, Joab raised no objections. He performed the task efficiently at the siege of Rabbah. Nothing could be cosier than David's response to the messenger, 'Encourage Joab and tell him not to be upset, since you never can tell who will die in battle. Tell him to launch a stronger attack on the city and capture it.' Later there had to be some tongue-in-cheek when he sent messengers to David to report: 'I have attacked Rabbah and have captured its water supply. Now gather the rest of your forces, attack the city and take it yourself. I don't want to get the credit for capturing it.' It clearly looks like a ploy to boost the king's credit and distract attention from his culpability in the case of Bathsheba.

RECOVERING THE WILL TO LIVE

See Chapter 22

David, it would seem, lost a decade to depression. It came in the wake of the prophet Nathan's prediction of trouble from his family (2 Sam. 12:11-12). He had plenty to underline what Nathan had said. His daughter was raped by her stepbrother, David's first-born. The firstborn was murdered by his younger stepbrother. This new crown prince exiled himself to a far country for three years and all that time David pined to see him.

Joab read the situation accurately and devised a way to shock the king out of his lethargy. He was very subtle. He did not tackle David directly. He found a wise woman from the countryside who was a good actor and storyteller. He devised a parable with strong religious overtones and with great sentimental appeal. He briefed the woman thoroughly and got her an audience with the king. The king fell for it, and as he did, sensed Joab's hand behind it. She admitted, 'It was indeed your officer Joab who told me what to do and what to say. But he did it in order to straighten out this whole matter.' 'Later on the king said to Joab, "I have decided to do what you want. Go and get the young man Absalom and bring him back here" (2 Sam. 14:5-24).

David's depression, however, lingered on for years. Psalm 143 comes from this trough in his experience, 'I am ready to give up; I am in deep despair. I remember the days gone by; I think about all that you have done, I bring to mind all your deeds. I lift up my hands to you in prayer; like dry ground my soul is thirsty for you. Answer me now, LORD! I have lost all hope. Don't hide yourself from me, or I will be among those who go down to the world of the dead.'

Not surprisingly, his treatment of Absalom provoked him to rebel and seize the throne. David retreated before him and slowly began to get back some of his old vigorous self. But Absalom was still an obsession, even after the rebels were defeated and Absalom was killed. He wallowed in his grief to the consternation of his soldiers. Again it was Joab to the rescue. This time the confrontation was open and direct. Joab told David to snap out of it and think of his own soldiers. It worked and Joab sparked again in David the will to live. This is probably Joab's greatest title to fame. It is difficult to imagine how David might have ended if it had not been for the blunt loyalty of his nephew.

A DIVIDED VISION

See Chapter 24

This time David tried, at last, to discipline his unmanageable Number Two. He dismissed him from his post as commander of the army. He promoted Joab's cousin, Amasa, who had actually sided with Absalom in the rebellion. It did not really make sense, although there might have been some short-term advantage in winning back some of the rebels.

Joab just bided his time. Amasa fell down on the job in the next insurrection and Joab slew him just as he had slain Abner thirty years before. What is significant, however, is the call that one of Joab's men made when the bleeding corpse of Amasa was lying like an ill omen in the middle of the road between two groups of soldiers. '"Everyone who is for Joab and David follow Joab!"... everyone followed Joab'. Who really was the leader, Joab or David? When a Number Two has a different outlook or vision from the boss, it makes it difficult for the followers. A divided vision leads to an ineffective team. Fortunately for David, Joab had no ambitions to be Number One. He was totally loyal even if he could not fathom David. When it is like this the people do not know who is leading and find it difficult to follow.

THE LORD YOUR GOD

Joab was not overly religious. There are just three occasions where God is mentioned by Joab. One was in the battle against Ammon where he assigned different tasks to himself and his brother. 'And may the LORD's will be done!' (2 Sam. 10:12). The second was when he put the words into the mouth of the wise woman of Tekoah in the parable she spoke to David. The third is the place where he really got it right and David could not see it in the matter of the census (2 Sam. 24:4-17). In trying to dissuade David he said, 'Your Majesty, may the LORD your God make the people of Israel a hundred times more numerous than they are now, and may you live to see him do it.' Notice, it was 'The LORD Your God' not 'The LORD our God'. It may well have been that to Joab kin was the motivating factor and not the Kingdom.

THE FINAL IRONY

Joab ended up being killed holding to the horns of the altar in the sanctuary. Late in the day and in a cowardly fashion, David decided that he had had enough from Joab, when he sided with his oldest son Adonijah in his bid for the throne when David was on his deathbed. Again there was ample reason for Joab to feel that he knew what David wanted. He was the oldest surviving son. David had been very indulgent to Adonijah and if David's behaviour to Absalom was anything to go on, it was likely that David would want him to have the throne. But he had not calculated on Bathsheba's influence and what nearness to death was doing to David's mind. He backed the wrong man and paid the penalty not just for that but for all that David harboured against him from the very beginning (1 Kings 2:5-6, 28-34).

So, he tried the religious appeal again. He clung to the horns of the altar. This time it did not work and he passed into history infamous rather than famous.

Just before I first became a Chief Executive Officer I learned an important truth. You get to the top by being very independent. The moment you get to the top you are totally dependent on those whom you lead. Make bad choices in those that you gather around you and it will damage the outcome.

TODAY'S CHALLENGE:

Ending well.

Paul said, 'the time is here for me to leave this life.
I have done my best in the race, I have run the full distance,
and I have kept the faith.'
(2 Tim. 4:6-7)

26
Leaving a Legacy

2 Samuel 23:1-7; 1 Kings 1–2; 1 Chronicles 22–29

THE SHORT STORY

There is a short and a long account of David's death. The short account telescopes and truncates what happened with an editorial policy that aims to elucidate the transition from David to Solomon, his son and successor. It describes an abortive coup when David was very old and how the parties who supported the coup were dealt with.

It would appear that this late act of disloyalty made David change his mind about his earlier policy of leniency towards his general, Joab, and the dissident Shimei from Benjamin. There is a healthy honesty in the way he spoke of this even if it was late in being expressed. 'He killed innocent men and now I bear the responsibility for what he did, and I suffer the consequences.' He charged Solomon to take his time, but to take them out when opportunity arose.

A TAINTED LEGACY

David laid on Solomon a very precise and recognisable charge about the way he should conduct his reign. It is reminiscent of the charge

Moses gave to Joshua centuries earlier, and indicates the real succession that David saw in the transition.

There is a certain irony in this charge. The reader cannot help being aware of David's own history in the individual matters he delegates to Solomon, and also his unspoken history. He did not have a clean record. He coveted, committed adultery and murder, and he womanised. He departed from the Law of Moses that forbade a king 'from marrying many wives, lest he turn away from the Lord'. David had married eight wives and maintained at least ten concubines. Solomon, in spite of this charge, married 700 princesses and kept 300 concubines (1 Kings 11:3). Many of them seduced him to worship other gods. David's words were great words. His example was a very tainted legacy.

THE LONGER STORY

This is in 1 Chronicles 22–29 and is more than three times as long as the 1 Kings ending. It was written a lot later, maybe centuries later. Israel and Judah had both gone into exile and only some from Judah had come back home after two generations. They were still a subject people. They had no king. They had their city back even if it was in ruins. They had a temple to rebuild. They also had their famous Law of Moses to relearn and uphold.

One of their number set about rewriting their history to put what they were trying to do in its proper context for the younger generation. One of his editorial policies was to show the nature and importance of the Temple. Of course, its beginnings were of very great interest when they were trying to put together the resources to rebuild it. We do not know what archives they had access to or how limited they were to anecdotal material, but clearly the story had to begin with David's capture of Jerusalem, his bringing the Ark to the city and the divine mandate for his son to build their central national shrine.

MORE VIGOROUS FINAL YEARS

The story of the Temple proper begins with the securing of the site (1 Chron. 22:1). This was also the jumping off-point for the shorter version (2 Sam. 24:25). The impression from Chronicles is that David was shocked into a new activism by his bad experience of the census and its aftermath. 'No time to lose!' seemed to be the motto. He nominated Solomon as the builder of the Temple (1 Chron. 22:6-10), and as he neared his end he made him king while he was still alive (1 Chron. 23:1).

Then he set about assembling materials, creating plans, recruiting workmen with every kind of skill, and assigning duties for the proper administration of life in this large and complex building and institution. He made provision for the offering of sacrifices, security, a school of music for the worship, record-keeping and supplies generally (1 Chron. 23:2–28:21). There is a hint that much of this activity might actually have been undertaken in the fortieth year of his reign when he was seventy years of age (1 Chron. 26:31).

A COMMITMENT TO EXCELLENCE

No one can read the lists of people, materials and duties in David's provision for the Temple without recognising a mind really given to plan, lead, organize and control work. Indeed if time is any test of a system, this was still operating, in part at least, 900 years later when Zechariah went up to the Temple just before Jesus was born (compare 1 Chron. 24:10 with Luke 1:5).

It is impressive also in that it is not just a list of names. People of ability are singled out, and recognized. The lists are peppered with phrases like, 'great ability', 'specially talented', 'highly qualified men for this work', 'a man who always gave good advice', 'outstanding men', 'outstanding soldiers', 'outstanding heads of families', 'Because of his skill in music, he was chosen.'

This is also evidence that the principle David enunciated when he bought the land from Araunah controlled everything that he did. 'I will not offer to the LORD my God sacrifices that have cost nothing.' In his own approach to music, the prolific production of psalms shows that he was part of this whole commitment to excellence and not just a watcher or a prescriber of rules for others.

A KINGDOM AND A MISSION

David bequeathed to Solomon a prosperous kingdom, beginning to be efficiently organized and effectively administered. From the River Euphrates to Philistia and the Egyptian border subject nations paid him tribute, and the people of Judah and Israel grew their grapevines and fig trees in peace, building on the foundation of his father's reign. Much more than the palace of cedar and marble, the treasury of silver and gold, the stores of olive oil and wheat, and the stables of chariots and horses, however, David bequeathed to Solomon a purpose and a mission: 'You must realize that the LORD has chosen you to build his holy Temple. Now do it and do it with determination' (1 Chron. 28:10).

Preparing for the Temple symbolised his devotion to God, an expression of love, a long overdue righting of the inadequate provision for the worship of God. Preparing for the Temple symbolized obedience to God's Law. David left Solomon his life's work.

THE GAPS

Where you fit in the shorter version of David's death in this later scenario is not clear. There is a hint that Solomon had a second inauguration (1 Chron. 29:22). It is difficult to decide which is the one that was sparked off by Adonijah. Indeed Adonijah and Amnon and Absalom and Tamar are all off the map as far as the Chronicler is concerned. The only place where they are mentioned is in the list of David's children (1 Chron. 3:1-9). Indeed the only mention of

Bathsheba is as the mother of four children she bore to David, one of whom was Solomon (1 Chron. 3:5).

A CONFIRMED COVENANT

The greatest gift that David handed on not only to Solomon, but to all his successors, has come to be known as the Davidic covenant. David instructed Solomon from his deathbed, 'Obey all his laws and commands, as written in the Law of Moses, so that wherever you go you may prosper in everything you do. If you obey him, the LORD will keep the promise he made when he told me that my descendants would rule Israel as long as they were careful to obey his commands faithfully with all their heart and soul, (1 Kings 2:2-4).

This conditional covenant depended on Solomon's obedience, but it was secured by God's promise. God had been faithful to David when he defended his father's sheep from the lion and the bear; faithful when he confronted Goliath with sling and stone; faithful when he ran from Saul's murderous spear and lived like an outlaw in the desert hills and caves; faithful when the men of Judah and Israel had made him king at Hebron; faithful when his army had captured Jerusalem and he had united the nation in the Holy City; faithful even when David had violated Bathsheba and suffered the punishment of Absalom's revolution. Confident now that the God who had been faithful to him all his life long would be faithful also to his descendants, David for the final time burst into poetic song to utter his last words:

> The spirit of the LORD speaks through me;
> his message is on my lips.
> The God of Israel has spoken;
> the protector of Israel said to me:
> 'The king who rules with justice,
> who rules in obedience to God,
> is like the sun shining on a cloudless dawn,
> the sun that makes the grass sparkle after rain.'

And that is how God will bless my descendants,
because he has made an eternal covenant with me,
an agreement that will not be broken,
a promise that will not be changed.
That is all I desire; that will be my victory,
and God will surely bring it about (2 Sam. 23:2-5).

Epilogue

There are arguments about whether public and private morality can be or should be distinguished from one another. David has showed us the way to get beyond and behind these distinctions and out of any confusion and dissonance they might bring.

HE STARTS AT A DIFFERENT PLACE

He starts with God who is above and beyond the world and everyone in it. He tries to think of his actions as he understands God thinks of them. At his mother's knee and in the sanctuary he had learned that God knows him inside out. There was no hiding from him. There was no gainsaying his judgment (Ps. 51; 139).

David was a normal person. He had innate selfishness, impulsive passions and stubborn reactions like the rest of us. Equally he had his better side and often it showed in his spontaneously acting on what he knew and had been taught.

Sometime he lost it completely. We had seen his lust and his lying; his complicity in murder and his susceptibility to taking revenge; his favouritism and the lottery that was his justice; his treachery and his massacres; his over confidence and his under performing. It is not a pretty picture. The text is no hagiography. David is no saint.

HE ENDED AT A DIFFERENT PLACE

Yet, these lapses, serious and without excuse as they were, were generally short lived. Both the historical text and his personal poems show him to be a man who owned up when he did wrong, sometimes before and sometimes after he was confronted about it.

What took him beyond any confusion about public and private morality was his understanding of the justice and mercy of God. God's justice both commended him when he did well and condemned him when he did not. God's mercy, when he found it again through repentance, transcended the wrong and moved him forward in God's unmerited favour.

David's Last Word

Happy are those whose sins are forgiven,

> whose wrongs are pardoned.

Happy is the one whom the LORD does not accuse of doing wrong and who is free from all deceit.

When I did not confess my sins,

> I was worn out from crying all day long.

Day and night you punished me, LORD;

> my strength was completely drained,

> as moisture is dried up by the summer heat.

Then I confessed my sins to you;

> I did not conceal my wrongdoings.

I decided to confess them to you, and you forgave all my sins.

So all your loyal people should pray to you in times of need;

> when a great flood of trouble comes rushing in,

> it will not reach them.

You are my hiding place;

> you will save me from trouble.

I sing aloud of your salvation,

> because you protect me.

The LORD says, 'I will teach you the way you should go;

> I will instruct you and advise you.'

Characters Around the Cradle

Witnesses to the Greatest Story Ever Told

Tom Houston

Tom Houston looks at a great story with a great cast: the political forces of Caesar Augustus; Herod and the travellers from the east; the religious establishment in Zechariah, Elizabeth, Anna and Simeon, the outcast prophet – John the Baptist; the ordinary people – Mary, Joseph and the shepherds; and also the Gospellers – Matthew and Luke.

ISBN 1-85792-755-9

Characters Around the Cross

Witnesses to the Cruxifiction of Christ

Tom Houston

In this updated and expanded version of the popular original, Tom Houston brings to life each of the characters involved in the death of Jesus on the cross. He provides us with insights into the historical context of each character and encourages us to imagine the impact that their encounter with Jesus would have had on their lives.

ISBN 1-85792-743-5

Characters Around the Church

Witnesses to the Birth of the Jerusalem Church

Tom Houston

The third in a series of Characters in the New Testament, this book looks at the birth of the first New Testament Church from the perspective of those who were there at the start - either helping or hindering the cause of the gospel.

The Twelve, Gamaliel, Saul, Herod Agrippa, Mary and Rhoda, Ananias and Sapphira are a few of the characters we meet in the book.

Tom Houston does extensive historical and biblical research for each of the chapters and you are guaranteed to learn something new about the beginnings of the gospel from this book.

Besides being an interesting read, this book is also designed to help preachers either prepare or present their sermons. There is an appendix on preaching bible characters.

ISBN 1-85792-803-2

Christian Focus Publications

publishes books for all ages

Our mission statement –

STAYING FAITHFUL

In dependence upon God we seek to help make His infallible Word, the Bible, relevant. Our aim is to ensure that the Lord Jesus Christ is presented as the only hope to obtain forgiveness of sin, live a useful life and look forward to heaven with Him.

REACHING OUT

Christ's last command requires us to reach out to our world with His gospel. We seek to help fulfill that by publishing books that point people towards Jesus and help them develop a Christ-like maturity. We aim to equip all levels of readers for life, work, ministry and mission.

Books in our adult range are published in three imprints.

Christian Focus contains popular works including biographies, commentaries, basic doctrine and Christian living. Our children's books are also published in this imprint.

Mentor focuses on books written at a level suitable for Bible College and seminary students, pastors, and other serious readers. The imprint includes commentaries, doctrinal studies, examination of current issues and church history.

Christian Heritage contains classic writings from the past.

Christian Focus Publications, Ltd
Geanies House, Fearn,
Ross-shire, IV20 1TW, Scotland, United Kingdom

info@christianfocus.com

For details of our titles visit us on our website
www.christianfocus.com